a New
Identity

Other books by Sheldon Charrett

Identity, Privacy, and Personal Freedom:
  Big Brother vs. the New Resistance

Secrets of a Back-Alley ID Man:
  Fake ID Construction Techniques of the Underground

Create a New Identity

Sheldon Charrett

THE MODERN IDENTITY CHANGER

CITADEL
PRESS

Kensington Publishing Corp.
www.kensingtonbooks.com

CITADEL PRESS BOOKS are published by

Kensington Publishing Corp.
850 Third Avenue
New York, NY 10022

All Kensington titles, imprints, and distributed lines are available at special quantity discounts for bulk purchases for sales promotions, premiums, fund-raising, educational, or institutional use. Special book excerpts or customized printings can also be created to fit specific needs. For details, write or phone the office of the Kensington special sales manager: Kensington Publishing Corp., 850 Third Avenue, New York, NY 10022, attn: Special Sales Department; phone 1-800-221-2647.

CITADEL PRESS and the Citadel logo are Reg. U.S. Pat. & TM Off.

First printing: May 2006

10   9   8   7   6   5   4   3   2   1

Printed in the United States of America

Library of Congress Control Number: 2005938600

ISBN 0-8065-2687-4

Contents

Warning

Certain passages in this book may reference laws in an informal and general manner. The publisher, author, and distributors of this book do not purport to be attorneys, nor do they advocate illegal activity. The information presented in this book should not be relied upon or used without first consulting an attorney and researching the applicable laws of the appropriate jurisdictions.

Some or all of the ideas presented herein may be considered illegal in many jurisdictions of the United States and elsewhere. This book is presented *for academic study only.*

Preface

There is a movement growing within the powers-that-be to stop books such as this from being published. There is at least one circuit court decision that has effectively banned certain types of controversial books by setting a precedent that allows crushing lawsuits against book publishers to go forward, even when such suits are based solely on the content of a published work. Our Supreme Court has refused to reconsider the matter.

Provisions of the so-called USA Patriot Act allow the government of our "free society" to demand customer book-buying and borrowing records from bookstores and libraries. These stores and libraries are prevented by the same law from revealing that they have even been approached by the feds, let alone let customers know that they are the subject of investigation.

Our legislators propose to narrow and qualify the First Amendment to the Constitution of the United States of America to suit their desire for control. This same movement believes that the United States should enact legislation mandating a national identity card as yet another means to track, keep tabs on, and otherwise invade the privacy of the citizens of our nation.

The traditional interpretation of the First Amendment allows any citizen of the United States of America to legally say, "I am John Doe," "I am Ghandi," or "I am God."

We, The People, intend to keep it that way.

Acknowledgments

I wish to thank:

Lisa Lisa.

My family and friends who have supported me. They are too many to list.

J.F., for his editorial support, kind words, and occasional bump in the right direction.

P.L., Paladin Press, and now R.E., Citadel Press, and the First Amendment to the Constitution of the United States of America, for giving this book a home.

Create
a New
Identity

Re-Introduction

It has been nine years since Paladin Press published this book's first edition. The Introduction to that text began with, "There is a silent, ongoing battle between the Bureaucratic Machine and those who oppose it." Any text acknowledging an "ongoing battle" demands revision after six years. Although most of my reader feedback remains positive, this past year especially I have seen an increase in requests to revise the original work. Therefore I present unto you the revised and updated edition of *The Modern Identity Changer, Create a New Identity.*

I have expanded the text from the original version by more than 10 percent and revised about 20 percent to account for six years of Big Brother's maneuvering. With such extensive revision and expansion, you may very well want to add this edition to your collection even if you own the original book.

A few years after this book's original release, I contracted with Paladin Press to write *Identity, Privacy, and Personal Freedom: Big Brother vs. The New Resistance.* That book is still in print, still selling well, and still available directly from Paladin. I mention it here because in many ways I'd always considered it a companion book to *Create a New Identity.* The text of that work delves more deeply into ways to protect your privacy without investing in a complete change of identity. Where appropriate, I will intersperse some of those ideas in this book.

READER FEEDBACK

This book's first edition was an instant best-seller. Paladin ordered a second printing within a week of the book's release to keep up with demand. I was thrilled, to say the least. Since its release, it has managed to remain on Paladin's in-house top ten list every sales cycle.

I do not let my head swell over this success, and I cannot take full credit for it. Even though it was my first published book, the credit for its success is owed to my readers. Before I wrote the book, I had a Web site (Web sites were known as bulletin board systems, or BBSs, back then), a small newsletter, and a discussion forum on the subject of identity change. The feedback from my early readers is what shaped this book.

As a best-selling book, it generated much more reader feedback than I ever had from my tiny grassroots newsletter and elite discussion forum. It is that reader feedback from the last six years that has shaped the revisions and expansions of this edition.

SEGMENTED IDENTITY

Readers' biggest concerns centered around the fact that the book implicitly recommended what some critics have called *segmented identity change*. This differs from the previous and more hopeful concepts presented in earlier texts such as *Paper Trip I* and *II*, where authors insisted that readers could slip into a total and complete new identity, starting over with a new Social Security Number, school records, driver's license, passport, etc.

The critics were right. The book did imply, and at times explicitly recommend, that a reader might wish to change only part of his or her identity to suit certain purposes. For example, if your only concern was ridding your life of junk mail, then perhaps all you needed was some useful tips on mail drops and how to eliminate your name from mailing lists.

Does this mean that in 2006 it is impossible to live under a complete new identity? Of course not. Is it more difficult now than it was when Barry Reid wrote the *Paper Trip* series? Of course it is. Big Brother *is* getting bigger.

To make it through every stage of a complete identity change without a glitch is rare. So this book, like the last, will be presented in such a way where the choice of segmentation is yours. What are your needs? How much are you willing to fight Big Brother? Only you can answer those questions.

CONCERNS FROM THE OTHER SIDE

Law-enforcement officers, politicians, and other conservative individuals who read the earlier edition also contacted me. They had many questions, but two were by far the most common.

Q. Who is this book for?

Actually, I couldn't blame them for asking this question. Although many how-to books have a "Who is this book for?" subsection somewhere in the beginning, my original did not. It was my first book. Maybe I was naive. I just figured it was for anybody who cared to read about the subject matter. Why not? Does a book *have* to be *for* someone?

Well, apparently to the control freaks among us, it does. And boy oh boy, if you don't say who the book is for, the controllers do indeed freak out. I have a whole file folder full of mail to prove it. So okay, okay already, I shall answer the almighty question.

A. This book is for . . .

The law-enforcement, politician, and conservative types who've pointed out the above "missing" subsection seemed to fill it in with their own paranoia. "Obviously your book is geared to the criminal element," wrote one enlightened politician. Others insisted that such books aided the underworld, the Mafia, drug traffickers, and even terrorists. Geeesh.

3

• ➤

Politicians fail to protect society because they are more interested in protecting their own. They cast about for scapegoats. I suppose it's easy for them to believe that drug kingpins, Mafioso, and international terrorists rely on "how-to" books to learn their trade. I'm not so sure they'll ever convince a street-smart and informed public of this illusion, however. "Hmmm . . . let's see . . . yes, that's the answer: If Paladin Press closed its doors tomorrow, I'm sure the most cunning criminals in the world would instantly be rendered impotent." Don't make me laugh.

I wondered: Did the "authorities" ever stop to consider that this book aided *them*? I mean, why were they reading it? Anyway, here's who this book is for:

- Anyone who's curious to learn how people change their identity.
- Screenwriters, novelists, and anyone in the entertainment industry in search of ideas and details for their stories.
- Abused spouses who have sought help from the system, only to be told nothing could be done until they or one of their children were injured or killed by their abusers.
- Victims of stalking or violent crimes.
- Witnesses left unprotected by the legal system.
- People in witness protection programs who don't completely trust the program.
- People with unwanted ties to the underworld who wish to free themselves of it but have no sympathy from law enforcement because of the very same ties.
- People falsely accused or wrongly convicted of crimes. NOTE: To date, Barry Scheck's Innocence Project has exonerated 86 wrongly convicted citizens of the United States, some of whom were on death row.
- People who have made mistakes, paid their debt to society, but still walk on unequal soil due to that black tattoo on their neck.

- Anybody who got scared after watching the video of the police gang-beating Rodney King with unnecessary weapons.
- People who have thoroughly studied history and see a grave disparity between the original intent of the U.S. Constitution and the present-day acts and resolves of the U.S. Congress and White House.
- Anybody with a lurking suspicion that those in power might favor their own interests over those of the general public.
- Anyone who enjoys reading controversial material simply because they have the freedom to do so and would like to keep that freedom alive.

Q. Why *not* have face recognition, surveillance cameras, and a national identity card *if you have nothing to hide?*

The "if I have nothing to hide" argument is so wantonly naive, it has always required the strictest composure on my part to address it without my blood pressure leaping to dangerous levels.

A. Quis custodiet ipsos custodes? [1]

First off, the phrase "I have nothing to hide" always implies, "I have nothing illegal to hide." But surveillance cameras cannot be programmed to capture only illegal activity. The cameras capture all.

Some corporations and bureaucracies are already arguing over whether surveillance cameras should be placed in employee restrooms. Proponents say that it will discourage long breaks, possible drug use, and even make sure employees wash their hands before returning to work. These are important matters, and, to some, the arguments even begin to sound reasonable after listening to them long enough. After all, if you're being a good boy and washing your hands after going potty, why not?

By this same logic, if you are a good prisoner of war, then you should have no problem having a serial number tattooed

• ✦

on your arm or a barcode on your neck. You have nothing to hide. You plan to behave according to the rules your watchers have set forth, and hell, isn't it better if they can identify you all the quicker as "one of the good ones"?

"But," cry the proponents of face recognition and national identity cards, "the comparison is unfair! The ink leaves a permanent mark on the prisoner!"

Seems like a good rebuttal on its face, but ask any Londoner whether the ubiquitous surveillance cameras of their city have left a permanent mark on them. In a recent study, London psychologists discovered that the city's use of surveillance cameras (several on every street corner) have had a profound and lasting psychological effect on its citizens. Londoners interviewed for the study said they felt they were never alone; that they were always being watched, even once they got home; and they were always looking to see who was looking. They said their behavior was affected by the expectation that whatever they did was being entered onto a permanent, videotaped record.

Are they kept more "in line" by their watchers? Probably. Are they living a human existence? Definitely not. Proponents of the "nothing to hide" argument completely fail to see that Big Brother robs the individual not only of the right to be individual but also of our most basic nature: that of being human, that of simply *being*.

THUS I PRESENT UNTO YOU . . .

I have presented the above as my best evidence of how my readers have influenced this revised and expanded edition, *Create a New identity*. The Bureaucratic Machine is getting bigger, but don't let the bastards hook you in. Don't let them sell you into loving Big Brother. When restrictive proposals are introduced by foolhardy legislators willing to sacrifice a pound of liberty for an ounce of perceived security, let them know what you think.

In an attempt to appease their subjects, many offices of the government have been forced onto the Internet to at least give the appearance of accessibility. Take advantage of this. When your congresspersons support bad bills, fill their e-mail inboxes with your thoughts! Take the runaway Information Age they've created and throw it right back at them! Set up your own Web site opposing them and exposing their folly. Fight the fingerprint! Preserve your right to burn a flag! Oppose the Patriot Act, which circumvents the First and Fourth Amendments! Oppose gun control! Let them know that We, The People, are STILL OUT HERE, and if they want to remain in office, they had best stop intruding on our liberties.

With this subtext strong in heart and foremost in mind, I now present the updated edition. The concepts within are intended to show how bureaucratic control over identity is the keystone that allows the arch of tyranny to remain forever suspended over our heads.

ENDNOTE

1. "Who is watching the watchers?"

Introduction

⮫.

I will not be pushed, filed, stamped, indexed,
briefed, debriefed, or numbered!
—The Prisoner

There is a silent, ongoing battle between the Bureaucratic Machine and those who oppose it. In their quest for privacy and personal freedom, free thinkers like identity changers have found it necessary to scrutinize the laws of our land and obey them to the extent that best preserves their personal liberties. In its quest to control the public, the Bureaucratic Machine churns out new laws that encroach on the liberty of free thinkers. For example, when our government first introduced the Social Security Number in the 1930s, concerns of the freedom-minded were allayed with promises that such a number would be used strictly as a retirement account number and never as a personal identifier. So free thinkers obeyed the law to its extent. When asked for their Social Security Number by bureaucracies unrelated to the Social Security Administration, free thinkers said, "No, thank you."

The Machine churned.

Now, a mere 70 years after those promises, a citizen can't do a damn thing without his state-issued serial number. Say, "No thank you," and they'll say, "No driver's license," "No bank account," or "No job." Today, people are serialized at birth, application for a Social Security Number being part of the maternity ward's routine paperwork. Tomorrow, the papers themselves will be supplanted by "smart chips" implanted in the back of baby's neck.

If you think that statement goes too far, think again. Today, new pets are being sold with chips in their necks for

9

• ➷

ease of identification. Now, imagine 250 years ago when this country was founded. Imagine a founding father proposing that each citizen be issued a serial number at birth. Imagine the gasp that would have echoed through the grand hall. Such a suggestion would have been unthinkable. The congressman's character would have been called into question. The rest of the assembly would have deemed the notion absurd.

Today, however, citizen serialization is effected without a second thought—not by the parents of the baby being numbered, not by the hospital administrators, and certainly not by any member of our swelling government. So, you are a number. How do you feel about that?

Many people feel the need to prove they are not a number by refusing to keep their "papers in order." Some people prove they are not a number by changing their number regularly; changing what our government considers to be their identity. They are known as identity changers, skin shedders, paper trippers, and new IDers. By any name, they are fighting an important battle.

Big Government and Corporate America need to be faced head-on. Identity changers find loopholes by familiarizing themselves with public policy and procedure. Bureaucrats fill loopholes by studying the habits of the individuals who live by them. This is how the battle is fought.

You do not want to use the information in this book with the attitude that you are "beating the system." Such an attitude could lead to trouble. This book does not teach you how to beat the system but rather how to play along with it and, hopefully, stay one step ahead of it. After you realize just where you stand, you will have a big advantage over the bureaucracies in that you can react to information much faster than can they. Government is too big. This is your advantage.

THE NEED FOR UPDATED SOLUTIONS

We recognize the battle and government's need to fill all loopholes. Therefore it stands to reason that identity changers must keep pace with updated solutions.

INTRODUCTION

Familiarizing yourself with such classics as *Paper Trip I* and *II* and other landmark books on the subject of identity changing is important and may also be of some benefit. Relying on these texts, however, is not recommended. Generally speaking, the serious identity changer should not rely on outdated materials. Published information that has been in the hands of government for more than a few years is likely to be obsolete. Although it is a sluggish bureaucracy, two years is more than enough time for the government and its various bureaus to recognize loopholes and fill them.

Clearly then, there is a need for updated solutions to the problem of identity changing. This book provides some solutions. Other recently published books on the subject of identity changing should also be consulted on a regular basis in order to keep one step ahead of the system.

PROBLEMS WITH PAST THINKING

Again, the basic problem with past thinking on identity changing is that it is no longer up to date. A technique, theory, legal loophole, or statement of law may no longer be accurate if it's learned from an old book. Some examples of past thinking that can lead a person into trouble include:

- The "infant death" method of procuring birth certificates
- Forged baptismal certificates
- Inventing Social Security Numbers
- The use of mail drops

Though all of these examples will be explored in this book, I will elaborate a bit here on the use of mail drops to illustrate my point.

It's easy to find published directories of U.S. mail drops that purportedly offer confidential mailing addresses for the purpose of achieving personal and financial privacy. The implication is that if a person were to acquire such a directory and take advantage of a listed mail drop, then personal and financial privacy would be attained.

Nothing could be further from the truth. As but one example, major credit bureaus maintain databases of known mail drops, which they routinely compare to credit applications and existing credit profiles. If your address matches one in the database, your credit report may be flagged for potential fraud. In fact, using published mail drops could lead an otherwise unsuspecting investigator right to your door.

Is this to say that one should not use mail drops? No. The trick is to know which ones to use—certainly not one that has been published in a directory, where the credit bureaucrats can get their sticky little fingers on it. If one were to purchase such a directory, it should be for the purpose of making sure a mail drop is *not* listed in it. So if you have a mail drop directory, it may still come in handy, although not in the manner you might have guessed.

Update on Mail Drops

Some of you reading this may know that the mail drop situation in the United States is not what it was when this book was first published. However, I left the above section mostly intact because it illustrates a point. Later in Chapter 4, "Establishing Residence," we'll really drive that point home when we talk about what has happed to mail drops over these past six years. In a word: devastation. But there is hope. Again, more on that later.

SUGGESTED READING

Regardless of the pitfalls with past thinking, a historical study of any subject is generally a good idea, and that tenet holds especially true for the subject of identity changing in America. If you're serious about following the suggestions in this book, then follow the first one: read these books!

- *New ID in America* by Anonymous (Boulder, CO: Paladin Press, 1983)
- *Reborn in the USA* by Trent Sands (Port Townsend, WA: Loompanics Unlimited, 1991)
- *Credit: The Cutting Edge* by Scott French (Boulder, CO: Paladin Press, 1988)
- *How to Beat the Credit Bureaus* by Bob Hammond (Boulder, CO: Paladin Press, 1990)

And, of course, from yours truly:

- *Identity, Privacy, and Personal Freedom: Big Brother vs. The New Resistance*
- *Secrets of a Back-Alley ID Man: Fake ID Construction Techniques of the Underground*

HOW IS THIS BOOK DIFFERENT?

This book does not spend a lot of time rehashing material that has been covered in other well-known books on the subject of identity changing. For this reason, it's assumed that you are familiar with most of the old ideas. For those who are not, the old ideas generally can be derived from the context of the situations and examples presented herein.

By studying past texts and keeping current with new ones, identity changers, freedom seekers, and privacy enthusiasts can maintain a fresh arsenal of information in the war against totalitarianism. We can then look our enemies confidently in the eye. We've said that Big Government and Corporate America need to be faced head-on, and this is how battles are fought. In the coming chapters, you will learn that, in fact, this is how battles are won.

CHAPTER ONE

What Is Identity?

⌣•

The answer is screaming at you loud and clear: you don't exist.
—Alan W. Watts

Webster's New World Dictionary, Third College Edition,
defines *identity* as:

- The condition or fact of being the same or exactly alike;
  sameness; oneness
- The condition or fact of being a specific person or thing;
  individuality
- The condition of being the same as a person or thing
  described or claimed

Expanding on these three distinct definitions, we can
demonstrate how society feels about identity. Different facets
of society have different attitudes about identity. Exploring
these attitudes will result in a more fundamental understanding of what identity is. You will then have a better foundation
from which to employ the material outlined in the chapters
that follow.

The first part of this definition describes how government
feels about identity. Government pulls its soldiers, police officers, bureaucrats, and taxpayers from a group of controlled,
unquestioning people. The government affectionately refers to
these people as "the masses." Certainly it is advantageous for
government to view the masses as having a uniform identity. It
is also advantageous for government if the masses view them-

selves as having one uniform identity. For example, the U.S. government is much more likely to enlist an "American" into the armed services than a recently married individual with newborn twins, a loving family, and a self-defined philosophy of life.

Government proliferates its concept of identity by touting police officers and military personnel as model citizens. Soldiers and cops who are injured in the line of duty become instant heroes. They are awarded medals of honor, given nice write-ups in the newspapers, and are often made the feature story on television news programs when nothing else is going on in the world. They are given nice disability pensions, and they spend their remaining years telling war stories as they unwittingly advertise government's position on identity.

The second part of Webster's definition describes people who do not fall victim to the attitude of the masses. These people are true individuals. They comprise the sector of society that thinks for itself. They are philosophers, artists, entrepreneurs, and people concerned with taking responsibility for their own existence.

This definition of identity describes who a person truly is. It is our self. It is who we were as a child, that same person we struggled with as a teenager, and, hopefully, the one we became as an adult. The unfortunate plight of the individual is that too many of us stray from ourselves once formal education is completed and the reality of survival in an economic society begins.

Throughout his trip through the government-sponsored school system, the student is taught that there is a very specific paradigm that must be followed in order to "survive" or "make it" in the world. The recommended program emphasizes (and even enforces if you try to educate your children in an unapproved fashion) many years of schooling, which will yield a certain understanding of society and the physical universe. Upon completion of education, one must find stable employment in order to support a lifestyle. Social interaction with the opposite sex is strongly promoted, and the expectation is to be married before age 30 and "settled down" with children in your own home shortly thereafter.

If this isn't enough to keep the masses busy, competition between members of society is continually promoted to ensure perpetuation of the rat race. Certainly, if Mr. Jones has a Saab 900, then Mr. Smith next door must purchase a BMW. If Mr. Smith sends his children to Harvard, then Mr. Jones must send his children to Oxford. The result is a society full of people obsessed with social status and having too many possessions that they never have time to enjoy.

Our identity, therefore, is reduced to our career and our rank in a material society. We dismiss that child we were as we grew up in exchange for the promise of social security, safety, and a few thousand dollars a year. In short, we accept the governmental definition of identity and live out a quasi-comfortable life of conformity and predictability.

Your quest to reestablish a relationship with your true identity has led you to this book. This statement may seem odd for a book written about changing your identity. Hopefully, though, you now see that it is the government's definition of identity that we wish to manipulate in order to preserve, or in some cases rediscover, our true identity.

Webster's third definition of identity, "the condition of being the same as a person or thing described or claimed," is the definition with which the balance of this book is concerned. We will learn to supply the bureaucrats with all their little papers, stamps, cards, and tracking numbers so that they leave us alone and instead hound some person who doesn't exist. In this way, we can be who we really are and do it on our own terms whenever we damn well please. When we need something from society, we simply present them with the appropriate documents and get whatever it is we need (e.g., employment, bank account, driver's license, Social Security, etc.). If they start to hound our "identity" too much, we simply change it. The system will then be sending mail and inquiries to an unresponsive void while the identity changer peacefully goes about his or her business.

Some may inquire, "Why not just stick with the identity I've had since birth?" If you can pull it off, that's great. My suspicion is, though, that if you're reading this book, you've already realized the overwhelming amount of information that the government has pertaining to the identity with which you were born.

The government starts tracking you from the moment you are born. It knows what time you were born, where you were born, how you were born, the names of your mother and father, the birthplaces of your mother and father, their Social Security Numbers, the name of the doctor who delivered you, and whether you were premature, late, or right on time.

When you were enrolled in school, the government started tracking your family's income, your medical history, your learning ability, your IQ, and your ability to conform. Remember those boxes on your report card? "Interacts well with other children." "Does what he/she is told." "Keeps his/her desk in clean condition." "Organizes work material efficiently." Everything is documented.

When you became a teenager, chances are that you were still too naive to know any better and, like most of us, willingly gave the government any information they wanted so you could drive a car or get a college scholarship. Perhaps you even thought about joining the army when you graduated from high school. Some of us actually did join the service. After all, we were trained 180 days a year to pledge our allegiance to the flag, and we were encouraged to join Cub Scouts or Girl Scouts and make our way through the ranks. If we were good enough, worthy enough, and loved our country enough, we became Eagle Scouts. We never bothered to stop and think about the words "scout" or "rank" or even "eagle." Sound like military terms, don't they?

There are other facets of your life that invariably become intertwined with your identity. Where you are geographically

situated is thought by many, especially marketing types, to be
a large part of who you are. Whether you buy into such things
or not, "social status" or your alleged "class" is thought to be
a determining factor as to the type of person you are. Where
you work, what type of work you do, the type of car you
drive, what kind of jacket you wear, and whether or not you
play bridge on the weekend are contributing determinants of
your identity as far as society is concerned.

The government desires to keep track of us in order to
keep us in its system. Many of those who begin to get ideas of
their own are offered high-paying positions in the government
and promised a pension when they retire. Most people jump
at this "opportunity" and are unwittingly swept into the system, regardless of their strong initiative and thinking ability.
The perks are hard to resist. And the more people beholden to
the government, the more people will tolerate one that contin-
uously grows in size and power.

Some of us have had run-ins with the law. Don't feel bad
if this has happened to you. Enforcement of the law is one of
government's favorite ways of keeping you down and busting
your self-esteem and sense of self-worth. Granted, we can't go
around slapping murderers on the wrist and telling rapists to
exercise self-control. Clearly, there is a need for laws in any
society. It is the abuse of the legal system to which I refer.

For example, cops love to chase teenagers out of the
woods and kick people off the beach. If you say too much
about the fact that it's a public beach, you dramatically
increase your chances of arrest. "I could arrest you for tres-
passing on public property, you know," says the enlightened
police officer. That's a good one. How can a citizen of the
public trespass on public property? But tell that to the cop and
you'll be sleeping on a cold metal bench that night. Drive too
fast or make a mistake on the road and you're pulled over,
detained, and fined, and your insurance goes up for the next
six years. Of course, any arrests, driving infractions, or subversive activity is noted on your permanent record. It is docu-

mented, stamped, numbered, filed, and added to the system's databases.

You've heard all the stories, so I won't bore you with them. The point is that government wants to keep you in line. If you fall out of line, you are made to believe it is because you have failed as a citizen. You are kept down. (What do some folks do who are kept down? They say, "Gee, I better go and join the army and get me some discipline or I ain't never gonna make nuthin' of myself.")

You can easily see how these experiences shape and mold us into what society says we should be. What we really are and what we really feel about any of it is of little concern to the bureaucrats who administer the system.

Now that you have a more solid understanding of the word "identity" as it pertains to this book, we can move on to discuss the various reasons for changing it.

CHAPTER TWO

Your Identity—Why Change It?

~.

. . . unhealthy aspects of speech, and dress not in accordance
with general practice . . .
—the Anarchists' consul,
from *The Prisoner*, final episode

There are countless reasons why an individual may wish to establish a new or secondary identity. Someone who desires to disappear altogether may have come to realize that life has simply lost its flavor. A person may one day wake up and realize that—through a lifetime of subtle changes in circumstance—he has become surrounded by people who do not fulfill him. He may ask, "How did I get here? Did I choose this life?"

Many people reassess their lives at some point, but even if they come to the above crisis, they resolve to simply get some new friends or sign up for new and interesting activities. Maybe they take up a new hobby or change jobs.

Those who desire to disappear usually have stresses in addition to a simple lack of fulfillment. On top of their emptiness, they may be overwhelmed by financial burdens that seem to never end. They may be haunted by a stupid mistake they made when they were young, maybe even a criminal conviction that keeps them from working in their chosen field, even though they have paid for their crime over and over again. Sometimes there are endless daily pressures that drive a person to desire a new life.

Other people may wish to establish a secondary identity, often for purely legitimate reasons. Maybe they sense the Orwellian trend of our government, and a lurking suspicion tells them they should construct an escape route just in case.

• ⤳

Some folks have realized that maintaining various aliases and identities enhances their personal privacy. Sometimes it's as simple as answering the telephone in a foreign accent or a child's voice to quickly deter invasive telemarketers. Or a person, especially a woman, may wish to give a false name and address when using the Internet to set up dates. Do you want a psycho date to turn into two years of stalking? An alternate identity is an easy way to avoid this.

Of course we must acknowledge that criminals, even terrorists, employ alternate ID to evade the law and/or to secure employment while in hiding. People opposed to published works such as this will immediately play the terrorist card. This is a poor argument. Criminals and terrorists also use automobiles, guns, GPS receivers, police scanners, flight training schools, public roadways, and Reebok sneakers to aid in their commission of unspeakable acts. Should we endeavor to ban all these things in the name of public safety, which we'll never have anyway, regardless of how hard we try? If someone is shot to death with a Glock handgun, shall we sue the oil company that distilled the diesel fuel used by the backhoe that dug the lead ore out of the ground from which the bullet was made?

That said, I would like to make it clear that this work is not intended to aid or encourage criminal activity. But we cannot ban alternate identification, even in the name of public safety. Many people who use alternate ID lead otherwise exemplary lives but may perhaps feel uncomfortable about purchasing certain products through the mail, such as this book. As stated above in my comments on the USA Patriot Act, our government tracks such things. If our government is allowed to meticulously serialize and scrutinize its citizens, and citizens have no way to sidestep Big Brother's gaze such as by using alternate ID, then the ultimate Orwellian nightmare will indeed manifest itself.

I must also note here that our government has no problem with using alternate ID for its own purposes. The federal government, especially, is responsible for thousands of identity changers who possess original-issue passports, driver's licenses, Social Security cards, and more, all sanctioned and securely backstopped by the very government that is so anxious to keep alternate ID out of your hands. You may be thinking I refer to the witness protection program, and that is, of course, one example. (I might also mention that participants in the witness protection program are some of the worst criminals this country has ever known: murderers, rapists, hit men, traitors, and terrorists.) But our supposedly anti-alternate-ID government also proliferates such documents for high-ranking CIA and FBI officials, so-called spies, ambassadors to Third World countries, former informants in the federal Witness Protection Program . . . the list goes on.

The reasons for new or alternate ID are as varied as the individuals who possess them. Some of these reasons may be "legitimate" in the eyes of society and some may not. It is not the purpose of this book to judge individual motives. I will elaborate on a few reasons, which range from purely innocent to what some might consider to be downright deceitful.

The reasons, though innumerable, do share one common tie—keeping ahead of the system. A growing number of people feel that government is too invasive, that we are looking down the throat of Big Brother, and our so-called privacy is quickly becoming a nostalgic notion. As you read through this book, you will begin to appreciate the constant tug-of-war that takes place as the system moves toward totalitarianism and a growing number of thinking people attempt to oppose, circumvent, and undermine this trend.

GENERAL PRIVACY

Changing your identity does not necessarily mean laser surgery, ties with the underworld, or taking four different taxis to work in the morning. Changing your identity could simply mean giving someone a fake name, address, and occupation. Certainly there are times when you are hesitant to give

CREATE A NEW IDENTITY

a store clerk your phone number. Never mind the near certainty of it being instantly forwarded to a marketing rep who will then call you that night during dinner—how do you know the clerk himself won't abuse it? Do you want to see his face framed in a pane of your bedroom window when you wake up the next morning? What about those lovely folks conducting polls or surveys? Do they really need to know who you are? Do you know who *they* really are?

How about dating? That can be risky business during the initial stages. Why offer complete strangers your real name and address? Remember the movie *Fatal Attraction?* If that's not a major incentive to keep your real identity private, then I don't know what is!

GOVERNMENT INVASION

The IRS (Internal Revenue Service, or "It's Really Slavery") now insists that all children listed as dependents or "qualifying children" on tax returns have a Social Security Number (SSN).

The Social Security Administration now indexes all "retired" SSNs in order to prevent unauthorized reuse of them. Quarterly circulars are made available to banks so that they may more easily recognize bogus SSNs.

Reciprocal agreements pertaining to the sharing of database information between state, federal, and private bureaus are being formed at an alarming rate. For example, child-support enforcement divisions now share information with public welfare departments to track the whereabouts of noncustodial parents (NCPs), *whether or not* the NCP is in arrears.

It gets better. DARPA (the Defense Advanced Research Projects Agency) is currently spearheading our government's most recent privacy monstrosity. The initiative, originally dubbed "Total Information Awareness" (TIA), was ostensibly spawned by the terrorist attacks of September 11, 2001. It's essentially a data-mining scheme, similar to those used by marketing agencies, except DARPA is injecting its version with heavy doses of steroids.

TIA would integrate computer access to existing and future-mined information of *every* United States citizen. This includes your private e-mails, credit card purchases, banking transactions, medical records, license applications, and driving record. Our government would be allowed to search these databases for signature patterns of potential terrorist activity. Nobody's talking about what these patterns might look like; defense executives just get a gut feeling such patterns must exist. It's something akin to *thoughtcrime.* I guess we may one day refer to it as *habitcrime* or *patterncrime.* Oh yes, did I mention these computer searches would be of the warrantless variety?

When privacy groups like EPIC and the ACLU reminded our government of a little thing known as the Fourth Amendment to the Constitution of the United States of America, they responded by crossing out the word "Total" and replacing it with the word "Terrorism."

Don't you feel so much better now?

Paranoid Government Bureaus

Any individual or organized group not conforming to a strict social code is labeled as radical, subversive, or militant. FBI files are started, certain persons and groups are targeted for surveillance, and, if the feds get too nervous, we have another Waco on our hands.

Profiling

Though we are supposed to live in a society where all men are created equal, where we are allegedly free to pursue life, liberty, and happiness, and where we are considered to be innocent until proven guilty, there are certain tactics used by government and law enforcement that make one wonder about the sincerity of all that.

For instance, the FBI, local police, and border patrols have established a system called "profiling." The system was initial-

• ✐

ly developed by a psychiatrist as a means of catching bombers and serial killers. The concept isn't a bad idea so long as its use is limited to catching existing felons who remain anonymous and at large.

The problem, not surprisingly, is that law enforcement has taken profiling to an abusive level. Hypothetical profiles of persons "likely" to commit a crime are now kept on file and, in fact, studied by law enforcement personnel.

If you're ever crossing the border between the United States and Canada, whether you're aware of it or not, your appearance is being judged and compared to profiles. There are so many people crossing the border that the border cops simply can't check all of them thoroughly. Ever wonder why some cars are searched more thoroughly than others? Profiles.

If you want an easy time crossing the border, you are best off driving a freshly washed late-model SAAB 900 with a clean interior, wearing a shirt and tie, and traveling with what appears to be a wife and two kids eagerly looking through sight-seeing brochures. The border cops will say, "You're all set. Have a nice trip."

However, if you're attempting to cross the border on a mud-spattered Harley Davidson, wearing your bandanna and a Grateful Dead T-shirt from 12 years ago, with a long string of multicolored feathers roach-clipped to your handle bars, you can expect a closer inspection.

The above is a somewhat diametrical example of profiling for the purpose of making a point. Some of you may say, "Yeah, no kidding. The dude on the Harley should be more suspect." Well, law enforcement takes this concept to extremes. According to their profiles, certain models of cars are more often driven by people who carry contraband and therefore more often searched. Certain ethnic groups are more likely to be drug smugglers. Certain hairstyles are associated with subversive activity. (Ever hear of skinheads?)

This is the essence of totalitarianism, my friends. The scary thing is that profiling is blindly accepted by most of society.

Face Recognition [1]

The Mandrake is a face-scanning system developed by Software & Systems in Slough, England. Surveillance cameras are set out at such convenient locations as airport terminals, train depots, shopping centers, and busy streets. The cameras are hooked up to computers that rapidly compare facial snapshots against a database of known and wanted criminals.

The system is fairly accurate. Since the device looks for skeletal patterns, it is not fooled by weight gain, changes of facial hair, or sunglasses. Since the skeletal structure of a human face does not change from age 13 to age 70 or beyond, Mandrake will not be thrown even by considerable aging. If your face is recorded in the Mandrake database, rightfully so or not, this device and the people using it can track you well into your old age.

When Mandrake finds a match, it audibly alerts the system administrator and places the suspect's picture at the bottom of a computer screen along with the database match. After recording the suspect's location, Mandrake continues to scan for other "criminals." If the system administrator confirms Mandrake's match, authorities can be dispatched to the suspect's location and, presumably, dragnet the area until the suspect is apprehended. Can you say *Orwellian nightmare?*

If an Inner Party member decides you are his enemy, he need only add you to this database to ruin your life. At the time of this writing, U.S. jurisdictions are testing this system and others similar to it. The word on the streets is that the bureaucrats love it. Big surprise.

The system is not completely accurate, and several matches may be produced for a given suspect. If you are an innocent person "caught" by Mandrake, a careless system administrator will dispatch authorities to come pick you up. If you are confused when they point their guns at you and you make the wrong move, such as reaching for your ID to prove your innocence, they will assume you are reaching for a gun and shoot you to death. Can you say *Ruby Ridge?*

• ✎

MAIL AND TELEPHONE PRIVACY

These days, most of the mail you get can instantly be placed in the recycle bin (unless you're really compelled to see exactly what the "Prize Notification Center" has sent). Most of the phone calls you get are equally useless, so here are some tips to take some power out of the hands of Corporate America and put it back in yours.

Want a quick way to sort your mail? Well, next time you're tempted by some piece of junk mail into ordering an "informative brochure," why not use an altered identity? By using a made-up name or, better yet, a misspelling of your real name and/or alteration of your address, you can easily identify all future junk mail that results from your responding to that one ad. Aside from the education that you'll receive regarding the marketing practices of Corporate America, you will gain the luxury of being able to sort your mail by subject simply by seeing how it's addressed.

For example, if you happen to reside at 180 Happy-Go-Lucky Lane and you become intrigued by the latest cure for baldness, respond to the ad using the return address 180B Happy-Go-Lucky Lane. Then, over the next 10 years when you are receiving junk mail from every bald scam in the world, you can throw it in the circular file as soon as you see the "B" in the address. This system works great for the individual with many interests. If you happen to be interested in art, boating, electronics, and music, you can reside at 180A, 180B, 180E, and 180M Happy-Go-Lucky Lane, respectively. The postman will still deliver the piece of mail to you as long as the altered name and address are close enough to the original.

You can employ a similar system for advanced call screening. If the voice on the other end of the telephone happens to be inquiring as to the availability of a Mr. Jonathan Dough, you can ask, "Is that Jonathan Senior, Jonathan Junior, Jonathan the Third, or little John-John? What is this regarding?"

"It's regarding that bridge in Brooklyn, sir."
"Oh, that'd be for Jonathan Junior. He just died."
"Okay, sorry to bother you." Click.

Magazine Subscriptions

Mail privacy also spawns another nice advantage for the information-savvy identity changer. If you have mutated your name enough and have enough distinct personal and business identities at your residence, then you can continually receive "free trial" issues of your favorite magazines year-round!

For example, if you happen to be interested in a magazine called *Identity Changing Times*, you could take them up on their no-obligation free trial offer. Usually, you can squeeze about three issues out of these offers before the company insists on your payment in order to "continue receiving the benefit of" reading their magazine.

So, if you've established four distinct identities at your residence, have each identity, in turn, accept the magazine's free trial offer and then cancel it after three months. State on the bill, "CANCEL. Do not want. Did not order." They are then obligated to cancel your subscription and stop billing you, but this doesn't always happen. Sometimes they keep sending you the magazine anyway. If so, it's yours to keep for free. They may send follow-up notices that purport to be "bills," but you don't have to pay them. Bottom line is that magazine publishers often prefer to keep you on their subscription list to impress their advertisers. After all, a magazine does not really make any money by selling subscriptions per se; the real money is in convincing advertisers that a lot of people read their magazine and thus the advertiser should spend their advertising dollars with that magazine. So when one identity has exhausted the free trial period, spark up number two. When number two has worn out his welcome, have one of your business entities receive the magazine for a while! (More on those business entities in Chapter 5.)

• ⤳

CHECKOUT COUNTER CARDS

Many grocery stores are now offering "special discount cards" that automatically qualify the user for in-store sales and specials. The user no longer has to cut coupons out and present them to the cashier in order to get a discount on their purchases. A variation of this is that the cardholder's total purchase price is discounted a certain percentage if they participate in the program.

Sounds like a bargain, right? After all, what do you have to lose?

I say that all you have to lose is your freedom, privacy, and eventually your sanity. What the grocery stores don't tell you is that the card is actually used to make a record of your buying habits, which is then exploited and sold to companies that compile mailing lists (see below).

Also, these cards will effectively determine just how much you are willing to pay for certain items. In this way, the merchant assures himself that he can squeeze every penny from you that he can.

These kinds of traps make it almost impossible to stay out of computer databases and off mailing lists. We've become an incredibly information-hungry world. Freedom-oriented people using alternate ID help fight this problem. My hope is that this book will eventually enable you to experience true personal freedom.

INFORMATION RESELLERS

Commercial information resellers make your personal information available to the general public. Items in these databases include last known address, mail forwarding address, magazine subscriptions, motor vehicle information, real property ownership, personal property ownership (such as mobile homes, watercraft, and aircraft), credit information, buying habits, average yearly income, number of children, marital status, court filings (including bankruptcies), judgments and civil filings, and much, much more.

BANKING PRIVACY

Among the more sophisticated reasons for establishing an alternate identity is that of financial privacy. If you happen to have judgments against you for unpaid taxes, it may be in your best interest to keep Aunt Hilda's generous bequest a secret from the rest of the world. Just exactly what are you to do with that $10,000 check from the law firm of Dewey, Fleecem & Howe? Well, you could deposit it into your savings account and wait for the IRS to seize it, or you could use the techniques outlined in the following chapters to hide your windfall. The choice is yours.

Hiding a bequest is one thing; keeping money from your child is something else altogether. Only you know if you're paying enough money to support your child. This book is not intended to provide a means for noncustodial parents to avoid financial responsibility for their children. (Granted, many custodial parents view child support as their livelihood and, unfortunately, many courts support this notion.) If you use the techniques in this book, be fair. Whatever you do, don't disappear on your children. The bond you can form with them is more valuable than any dollar amount society can take away from you.

Running Scams
As mentioned before, this work is not intended to encourage or assist illegal activity. But in fairness, we must admit that alternate identities can be abused.

Planning on hitting up some nice credit card companies for some play money? Or maybe ordering up some utility services on the cuff for a year or two? Whatever your game, you probably won't go around flaunting your real name, address, and credentials—unless you're just in it for the short term and anxiously looking forward to some "time off" at the county's expense.

When the credit card company begins to wonder why you haven't made any payments toward your $7,500 in recent charges, you deem it better that they go pounding on the door of a mail drop rather than your own. When the cable police show up to snip your wire and grab their box, it would be nice if you could simply smile and say, "Oh, that bastard. Yes, my landlord had a bitch of a time getting him outta this place. Matter of fact, I was supposed to move in a month ago and that SOB held me up. If you do find him, tell him that I'd like to have a word with him. Cable box? Don't see one here. Go ahead and snip away, though. The irony is, I was just going to call up and order some cable myself. Sure you want to snip that wire?"

Ah, the silly games people play.

PURCHASING ALCOHOL

Perhaps one of the most popular reasons for obtaining counterfeit identity documents is for the purpose of procuring alcoholic beverages. Young adults are naturally curious about things, especially those that society says are off-limits. So, when a minor is slightly shy of the legal drinking age, the natural desire is to obtain ID that says otherwise and find out what alcohol is all about.

Young women can often get away with using their older sister's driver's license to get into nightclubs. Of course, young men can also borrow their older brother's ID to get into nightclubs, but this trick doesn't work as well for men.

There are a few reasons why women are more likely to experience success when borrowing an ID. For example, women are known, in fact expected, to change hairstyles and appearance often, sometimes on a daily basis. Therefore, when presenting her older sister's ID, a woman does not necessarily have to look exactly like the photograph on the ID.

Oftentimes, it is not even necessary for a woman to use the ID of a relative. Women who hang out in cliques often resemble each other to a great extent. If one woman is of legal drinking age, she can enter a nightclub and pass her ID back to an underage member of the group who resembles her. The underage woman can then reuse the same ID and get into the club. I've seen this done more than once.

When an underage male tries to present his older brother's ID at a bar or nightclub, he comes under much more scrutiny. A major reason for this has to do with the late maturity age of adolescent males. Many males between the ages of 17 and 19 still look like kids. When they attempt to use their older brother's ID, the photo may contain telltale signs that the bearer is not the person in the photograph. For instance, the older brother's photo may depict a post-adolescent male bearing a five-o'clock shadow and clear complexion. The younger brother using this ID may lack significant facial hair and have an acne condition. This will cause the bouncer to send him on his way.

• • • • •

Now that we've enumerated some reasons for wanting an alternate identity, we can discuss some ways to accomplish this. We will begin by identifying the various ID documents. Then we'll discuss how to acquire or manufacture them.

ENDNOTE

1. The first half of this section is taken from *Identity, Privacy, and Personal Freedom: Big Brother vs. The New Resistance,* by Sheldon Charrett, Boulder, CO: Paladin Press, 1999.

CHAPTER THREE

Identity Documents

⌒.

*A National ID Card is not really about identity. It is about
authorization . . . [The ID will be required] for the purchase
of alcohol, tobacco, prescription drugs, firearms, ammunition,
knives, fertilizer, flying lessons, or any other goods or services
the government considers dangerous . . . When you present
your National ID to complete a transaction, you will actually
be asking the federal government for its permission.*
—Duncan Frissel

We all know who we are. But how do we show others
who we are? To a certain extent, others can see who we are.
To most people, it is readily apparent if we are male or
female. We are observably tall or short. Our racial origin is
easily determined and, in some cases, our ethnic background is
there for the world to see.

However, it is not readily apparent if someone is, say, a
certified public accountant. Of course, I could tell you that
I'm a CPA, and you may accept this. Chances are, though, if
you were running a business and wanted to hire me to do
your books, you would expect me to validate my claim that I
am a CPA. In anticipation of this, most CPAs hang their certi-
fication in a frame on their office wall. This example demon-
strates that, in society, identity documents show others facts
about ourselves that others may wish to know.

Sometimes, though, people "wish to know" more than we
care to tell them. Brushing them off is, at least, uncomfortable
and, at worst, the beginning of a heated argument. Fortunately, the identity changer has documents and tactics to help

• ➤

avoid such unpleasantries. In this chapter, we will explore how to obtain identity documents and how to use them to protect your privacy.

PART ONE: READILY AVAILABLE DOCUMENTS

An identity document is nothing more than a device used to demonstrate to another individual that you are who you say you are. In our society, there are a certain number of items that people typically use to accomplish this. The type of identity document necessary to perform the task will vary depending on whom you are trying to convince and of what you are trying to convince them.

Recently, I had accepted an offer from a certain manufacturer of postal metering machines. The offer allowed me to try their machine free for three months. If, after three months, I decided that I didn't want to keep it, they would come pick it up and I would be under no further obligation.

So, I tried the machine out. After the free trial period, I decided that it would not be worth the rental expense. Accordingly, I called the company and, a week or two later, two servicewomen showed up at my office to remove the machine.

Being a cautious individual, I asked one of the women if she had anything on her which would indicate that she was, in fact, a representative of the company in question. She showed me her clipboard, which contained a professionally printed invoice from her company that included my name, address, and account number. She then insisted on showing me her driver's license. I told her that that was not necessary but nonetheless, she showed it. Shortly afterward, I carried the machine down to their truck, which had other machines from the same company in the back. I signed a few papers, got a receipt, and the transaction was concluded.

Reflecting upon this afterward, I thought it somewhat ironic that the girl insisted on showing me her driver's license. First of all, it was a testament to the fact that the driver's license has become the standard piece of "concrete" identification in the United States. The irony was that her driver's license in this particular instance was of little or no import. What I needed to know as a consumer was if I was releasing this expensive piece of machinery to the proper individual—the proper individual, in this case, being a representative of the company that owned the machine. As it turned out, the invoice and the other postal metering machines in the back of her truck were the "identification documents" that convinced me she was who she said she was. Her driver's license alone would not have accomplished this.

Of course, had she been a con artist, the "identifying documents" in question (i.e., the invoices and postal metering machines) would have been fine examples of identity documents that are ridiculously easy to obtain, however specific to the cause they may have been.

I would like to begin our discussion of available identity documents by discussing other, more general, examples of such documents that are extremely easy to acquire.

DRIVER'S LICENSE: DON'T BE A FOOL, GO TO SCHOOL!

In the United States, the driver's license has become the foremost means of positive identification. For the serious identity changer, a valid driver's license is an invaluable tool to have. Your new life will be so much easier once you possess one. However, obtaining a driver's license under an assumed identity is not as simple as walking into the Department of Motor Vehicles and getting your picture taken. The process involves obtaining a learner's permit (in many states), "learning" to drive for a period of at least six months, passing a written exam, and then taking a road test.

The advantage here is that so much emphasis is placed on verifying the road knowledge and driving skill of the applicant, there is much less emphasis on verifying his or her identity. The disadvantage is that there's a considerable amount of time involved and, in some states, the applicant must have a licensed driver accompany him or her during the road test. If you are planning to make a clean break, you probably don't want to enlist one of your friends to accompany you during your road test. Your friend will be wondering why you are taking the test when he's always known you as a licensed driver. He may also be curious as to why the examiner keeps calling you "Mr. Capone."

A parsimonious and elegant solution to this dilemma is to enroll in a driver's education program with a driving school. If you happen to be much older than your late teens or early twenties, it will look much less suspicious if you do this in an urban area. Due to the availability of public transportation, many folks who live in urban areas do not learn to drive until they are much older, if ever. To some, the entire process of enrolling in a driver's education program, attending classes, taking one-on-one driving instruction with a trainer, and then going for the "big day" to get a license may seem somewhat elaborate. But that's exactly the point. It's so elaborate that it shields your actual intention quite well. Besides, it's a lot easier to lie to a driving instructor than to a registry cop (most of the licensing preliminaries will be handled by the driving school).

CREDIT CARDS

Anybody who has a nicely manufactured ID (see Chapter 6) and a Visa, Mastercard, or American Express is obviously a stand-up citizen and deserves a minimum of fuss when, for example, opening a checking account. (Details of opening a checking account will be presented in Chapter 7.)

But you can't get a credit card without proper credit, right? Wrong. When it comes to acquiring a clean credit card, there are two big loopholes that can be useful to the identity changer.

One convenient loophole is the secured credit card. A secured credit card is one where the cardholder uses a bank deposit as security, or collateral, against the card balance. If the cardholder skips town, the credit card company can seize the bank balance to pay off the cardholder's debt. Credit card companies, being greedy entities, will typically solicit secured accounts from individuals with poor credit or no credit at all. Of course, if you have good credit you can also get one, but why would anybody want to do that?

The safest way to do this is to establish a credit profile on the new "you" by using the techniques outlined in Chapter 8, then wait to be added to the mailing lists of secured credit card companies. An equally safe way is to call up such a company and ask them to send some literature and an application to your new address. WARNING: Do not do this from your old address, your old employer's address, or from anywhere connected with your past life (e.g., the address of a friend, relative, girlfriend, cell mate, etc.). Make sure that it is the "new you" making the call and giving the address and phone number of your new identity. Caller ID is a favorite database builder and fraud detector among banks and credit card companies.

(Credit card companies require you to call an 800 number to verify that you received their credit card. The computer system answering the phone first tries to verify that the telephone number you are calling from is the same number you gave as your home phone number on your credit application. If it is, you are then required to punch in your Social Security Number and perhaps some other verifying information about yourself, such as your mother's maiden name. If the number you're calling from cannot be verified as your home number, the computer system generally gives you the message, "Your call is being transferred to an account representative," or something of that nature. The representative will ask questions of a more scrutinizing nature regarding your identity, as a flag for potential fraud has been raised. Be forewarned!)

Another way to obtain a credit card as ID is to add a cardholder to your existing account. Of course, this account must be in good standing and stay in good standing throughout the process of spawning a new credit profile. American Express is the best company for doing this because it maintains its own credit database and is exceptionally hungry for information. AMEX insists on having the new cardholder's Social Security Number so that it can start up a profile on that person. (Acquiring a new Social Security Number will be discussed later in this chapter.)

This will get you three things for the person you wish to create: a piece of identification; a credit profile established with AMEX, which is eventually sent out to credit information services such as Experian; and, most importantly, a good credit history transferred to the new you.

Why is this important? Well, the new credit profile will state that "another party is liable for this account." However, if all payments are made on time, the owner of the new credit profile will eventually start receiving preapproved credit card offers. The time frame for this is usually 6 to 18 months. When this happens, accept the preapproved offers and immediately stop using the first credit card altogether. Also, the "old you" should cancel the credit card originally used to spawn this credit profile after it's been completely paid off. The sooner the original credit card company shreds your files the better.

This is all beautiful, right? Well, that depends on just why it is you want to create this new person (see Chapter 2). If your intent is to get lost forever, do not use this approach. While it is certainly feasible that the connection between your "real" credit profile and the new credit profile may eventually be buried so deep as to render it economically unfeasible for anybody to bother to trace, it is not a clean break! When you use the new credit card to open a checking account under your new identity, the clerk may make a photocopy of your ID as well as a memo of the account number imprinted on the credit card. This loose thread back to the old you is not the kind of thing you want to have floating about in cyberspace.

Again, if the new you stays clean, you may never have a

problem. But consider your sanity. When you make a break, you want to make a clean break. Otherwise, you will always be wondering if someone has used such loose ends to track you down. What if, for example, somebody hired a private investigator to find you? With that credit card connection, he or she would be able to find you quickly. You will always have that insecurity in the back of your head. Isn't this what you were attempting to get away from to begin with?

SOCIAL SECURITY CARD

Once you decide on which Social Security Number to use for your new identity (see Part Three of this chapter), you can then deal with the relatively simple process of producing the Social Security card. The insignia on your typical Social Security card consists of an American bald eagle holding a box in which your SSN is printed. There are lots of companies around that will print your SSN, or any SSN, on such a card for a nominal charge. Or you could always photocopy someone else's card, white-out their SSN and type in your own, then photocopy the amended card and laminate it. Color copies work best with this approach.

Be aware that the Social Security Administration (SSA) now uses security paper, which cannot be properly photocopied. Old-style cards still work nicely. If you manufacture one based on the old style, be sure to dog-ear the corners and dust your TV with it so it looks as old as you're claiming it is.

Here is a favorite trick of mine. Ever see those life insurance companies that offer you a nice Social Security card with your number on it simply for requesting their information packet? The offer does not even need to be addressed to you! Simply fill out the information request form with the desired name, address, and SSN. The company will be happy to add you to its database, and you will receive a nice, credit-card-sized piece of plastic complete with the eagle insignia, your name, and your SSN. This adds a nice touch to your portfolio of identity documents. This will also place you on a few junk mailing lists, which is a nice additional benefit if you have a mail drop and you want your flow of mail to appear ordinary there.

PHONE, ELECTRIC, AND GAS BILLS

Though not normally thought of as identity documents, there are a few times when these little buggers can come in handy. When relocating under a new identity, you will undoubtedly have your utilities turned on in your new name at your new address. Chapter 4 enumerates the different options an identity changer should consider before establishing a new residence. Your need, or lack of need, for utility bills will of course factor into your decision. Obviously, you can't turn the electricity on in a mail drop. Also, answering services do not bill you the traditional way in which the telephone companies bill you.

As you will learn in Chapter 4, having a phone in your own name often gives you an edge when applying for credit. Moreover, you will find that it is very difficult to order a copy of your credit report without proof of address. Usually, the credit reporting agency will readily accept a utility bill as proof of address.

Another instance where a utility bill comes in handy is when opening bank accounts. One bank I deal with will not open a bank account for you unless you present two forms of identification. One, they say, must be a driver's license and the other a utility bill. I went so far as to ask the accounts manager if a credit card or birth certificate would do. The answer on both counts was "no." Granted, you could make a big stink about how you don't drive, never did as a matter of fact, and while we're on the subject, I don't believe in electricity; oh, and by the way, I'm part Amish, and isn't there some law against this? Eventually, they will grease you so you don't squeak, to borrow from the old adage. But do you really want to generate that kind of attention when opening a bank account under an

assumed identity? If they give you a hard time, simply go elsewhere. Or, if you happen to have the necessary documents . . .

Also, utility bills, when strategically deployed as innocent
trash on the backseat of your car or on the front and back
dashboards, make for much less question answering during
routine traffic stops, if you catch my drift.

Of course it never hurts if you just happen to be carrying a
bunch of bills that need paying when, let's say, you're stopping
by the local Social Security office, county clerk's office, or vital
statistics registry. Placing them innocently on the counter at a
convenient angle while speaking with the clerk will provide an
excellent subliminal base from which you can manipulate your
friendly bureaucrat. Of course, "manipulate" is meant in the
most loving, humanitarian sense of the word.

BAPTISMAL CERTIFICATE: DON'T EMBARRASS ME!

Several books on the subject of identity changing seem to
hail the baptismal certificate as some type of boon to those of
us interested in changing our identity. This notion had some
merit many years ago when the system was experiencing true
prosperity and fewer of us had to resort to tricking it to make
a buck. These days, the baptismal certificate simply doesn't
fly. The Social Security Administration won't even accept a
baptismal certificate as secondary ID. Its application states
that it will accept a "church membership or confirmation
record (if not used as evidence of age)." That's as close as they
get to accepting a baptismal certificate.

Despite my skepticism, I thought that I'd lend this baptismal certificate enough credence to actually conduct some
field research on the matter. To make the experiment as sound
as possible, I used my actual baptismal certificate as opposed
to a forgery or reprint. My mother pulled it out from my
"Baby Days" book, where it had been stuffed decades ago and
hadn't been seen since. I attempted to use this form of identity
in the following situations:

- Purchasing alcohol
- Entering a club
- Cashing a check
- Using a credit card

Now tell me, how many strange looks did I get that day? Have you ever carried around your baptismal record as proof of identity? Think about it.

LIBRARY CARDS AND FINISHING TOUCHES

Sometimes referred to as "ancillary documentation," lesser forms of identification should not be taken lightly. Aside from a driver's license, credit card, and Social Security card, most people have other forms of ID in their wallets. Since most folks don't consider these other documents as being identification, it is very easy for the novice identity changer to ignore having them in his possession. However, if all you have is a brand-new driver's license, credit card, and Social Security card in your wallet, most bureaucrats would find this highly suspicious. So scuff up that license, send that Social Security card through the wash a couple of times, and get some use out of that credit card. Then, begin collecting some of these "lesser" forms of identification:

Wallet Insert

This one's a gimme—it comes with the wallet. What more could you possibly ask for? Fill it out with any specifics you desire. For example:

Dr. Larry C. Fine
123 Stooge Terrace
New Rochelle, NY 10017
"Reward if found and returned intact."

For an extra special touch, add the monogram LCF to the wallet!

Library Card

You really should have one anyway. It's probably not a good idea to use your old one while living under a new identity. In fact, it's probably a good idea to have a few library cards under different identities, depending on what you're into.

Ever see the movie *Seven*? There was a scene where the cops were out of leads and the bad guy was about to get away. (Sounds like a lot of movies, doesn't it?) So, the senior cop on the case examines the perpetrator's modus operandi. It turns out that the perp is seeking out the most egregious violators of the seven deadly sins, torturing them for extended periods of time, and finally executing them. The senior detective can see by the perp's MO that he possesses a great deal of knowledge pertaining to certain cult activities and decides the guy must be frequenting the library for reference material. He then informs the junior detective about a secret FBI database. According to the senior detective, the FBI targets certain literature in the library and tracks the name and address of any patron checking out the material. Apparently, how-to books on such topics as making explosives, screwing the government, the ins and outs of counterfeiting U.S. currency, identity changing, and the like are not favorites of the FBI.

As mentioned in this book's preface, provisions of the USA Patriot Act allow the government to demand customer book buying and borrowing records from bookstores, publishers, and libraries. These stores, publishers, and libraries are prevented by the same law from revealing that they have even been approached by the feds, let alone informing customers they are the subject of investigation.

The truth is actually stranger than fiction. So if you don't want Big Brother to know your reading habits, get a library card under an assumed identity.

Tax Documents

Tax documents, especially between January and April of any year, also make very convincing quick-and-dirty identification.

Simply tell the IRS you run a business and need W2 and 1099 forms. They will send you lots of blanks, which you can then fill out in any name you want. You can even have a W2 issued to your alias who happens to work for any company you'd care to invent, even the IRS. One of these folded up in your wallet, or conveniently left on your car seat, or mingled with your papers during a job interview, can often come in handy.

Jewelry, Jackets, and Laverne and Shirley

A few ornamental things can help to wrap up a new identity. By using engraved jewelry, class rings, monogrammed articles of clothing, and accessories, the identity changer can complete the image of being who he says he is. If you are going to be Buffalo Bill for a few years, it's a nice touch to get a windbreaker with "Buffalo Construction Company" embroidered on the back of it. This is much better than simply wearing a nametag that says "Buffalo Bill." Also, if you happen to be calling yourself Billy the Kid these days, it doesn't make a whole lot of sense to be wearing a jacket that explicitly states you are, in fact, Doc Holliday.

In the real world, people do things. They have businesses and hobbies, play sports, or are otherwise enthused by cars, motorcycles, roller coasters, or pig farming. Most people work their identity into what they do. They don't even think about it. So, instead of just saying that you are indeed Mack the Knife, you will make a better impression by wearing a 1920s black sharkskin suit and keeping your teeth real white.

Let's not overdo it, though. If you walk into a bank and you have the Elvis tattoo, necktie, necklace, bracelet, jacket, monogrammed wallet, guitar sack, and secret decoder ring, the effect may turn out to be the opposite of what you'd intended.

I once heard it said that we all know what the "L" stands for on Laverne DiFazzio's sweater in the 1970s sitcom *Laverne and Shirley*. This is a fine example of mixing subtlety with high visibility.

~ •

PART TWO: BIRTH CERTIFICATES

Before delving into the logistics of whose birth certificate you should be obtaining, we should first discuss how easy it is to get a certified copy of any birth certificate your identity-changing heart desires. Every U.S. state or commonwealth, including Washington, D.C., has at least one registry of vital statistics. The vital statistics office is the central clearinghouse for all birth, marriage, and death records on file in every county in that state. The atmosphere at your average vital statistics office is pleasantly bureaucratic, and I strongly suggest patronizing it when you finally decide who the hell it is you want to be.

Why go to the big, scary, bureaucratic state agency instead of to the town or county clerk? Well, two reasons immediately come to mind. One, at the state level it's less likely that the bureaucrat will have personally known our deceased subject. Certainly, we would not want to walk into the town clerk's office professing to be Iggy Piggy and demanding his birth certificate, only to glance down at the clerk's nameplate and see "Iggy Piggy, Senior—Town Clerk" forbiddingly engraved in low-grade aluminum.

Secondly, you will have a strong psychological advantage when dealing with the predictable state bureaucrat. Since you know certain things about his behavior—specifically, his desire to both exercise power over you and brownnose his superiors by selling you something you don't need and thus making a quick $6 for the state—he can be manipulated easily.

I will show you how this works by first demonstrating how it doesn't work. If you definitely want to get a hard time, try this approach. Go into your state's vital statistics office and say, "Hello, I would like a certified copy of Iggy Piggy's birth certificate, please." A typical response from the bureaucrat would be, "Why? Who the hell are you? Are you Iggy Piggy? Why do you want a certified copy of his birth certificate?" Of course, the birth certificate is a public document, but try telling this to the bureaucrat.

Now try it using what you know about the psychological makeup of the typical bureaucrat. Walk up to him meekly and act stupid so he will know how superior he is. Say, "Um, I was just doing some genealogical research and I found a birth record that I would like a plain photocopy of." He will respond in a superior tone to show you how little you know, "We can't issue photocopies. We only issue certified copies at a charge of $6 per copy." You then respond, "Golly, well I'm new at this. There's really no other way?" He will educate you by telling you that of course there is no other way; we just can't go issuing photocopies of birth certificates with all the fraud that goes on these days, you know. With that you simply respond, "Oh, well I guess if there's no other way, I'll have to pay the fee. Hopefully my client will understand and reimburse me." You will have a certified copy of "your" birth certificate in a few minutes at a fee of roughly $6 to $12 in most states.

There are certain situations where a person might desire a certified copy of a birth record for someone who doesn't exist. Or maybe you just don't feel like paying $6 to $12 to get one for somebody who does exist. Chapter 6 of my book *Secrets of a Back-Alley ID Man: Fake ID Construction Techniques of the Underground* contains a step-by-step procedure for constructing a state's "long form" certified birth certificate complete with a raised (embossed) seal. *Back-Alley ID* also has techniques for reproducing city-issued, card-sized birth certificate abstracts, which most people carry in their wallet.

PART THREE:
THE SOCIAL SECURITY NUMBER

Several books on the subject of identity changing consider the birth certificate to be the "cornerstone" or "benchmark" of a person's identity. In my entire adult life, I have yet to have a bureaucrat request my birth certificate as a form of identification. Granted, for certain key documents such as a driver's license or

Form R-56
50M-8/95

The Commonwealth of Massachusetts
EXECUTIVE OFFICES OF HEALTH AND HUMAN SERVICES
STATE DEPARTMENT OF PUBLIC HEALTH
REGISTRY OF VITAL RECORDS AND STATISTICS

A 012345

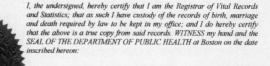

I, the undersigned, hereby certify that I am the Registrar of Vital Records and Statistics; that as such I have custody of the records of birth, marriage and death required by law to be kept in my office; and I do hereby certify that the above is a true copy from said records. WITNESS my hand and the SEAL OF THE DEPARTMENT OF PUBLIC HEALTH at Boston on the date inscribed hereon:

DAFFY D. DUCK
Registrar

IT IS ILLEGAL TO ALTER OR REPRODUCE THIS DOCUMENT IN ANY MANNER

My book *Secrets of a Back-Alley ID Man: Fake ID Construction Techniques of the Underground* shows how to make this state "long form" certified birth certificate template. Place it in the paper tray of a photocopier and copy a real birth certificate that has been altered to your heart's desire.

• ⤳

passport, a birth certificate is needed during the application process. But for day-to-day living, it is the Social Security Number that is most often requested by banks, credit card companies, police departments, municipal offices, motels, automobile rental agencies, and just about anybody who wants to keep tabs on you.

Like everything else bureaucrats desire to keep track of, human beings have been serialized. Once established, your SSN is the serial number that stays with you for the rest of your life.

A BRIEF HISTORY

United States Code Title 42, Section 301 *et sequentia* brought the Social Security Act into existence in 1935. The program was allegedly established as a kind of forced retirement plan to provide for the general welfare of individuals who reach the age of retirement or become disabled and can no longer provide for themselves.

Under the plan, all individuals deriving income from salary, wages, tips, commissions, or self-employment must pay a portion of their earnings into a Social Security account. Each wage earner has a unique account with the Social Security Administration (SSA), which is identified by his SSN.

The SSN is used to keep track of an individual's earnings on a quarterly basis. Upon a person's disability or retirement, the records are used to determine the dollar amount of monthly benefits that will be paid to the individual. In short, the more you pay into Social Security, the more you will get when you become eligible to collect benefits.

Regulations were also promulgated relative to the issuance of Social Security cards and the order in which SSNs should be assigned. It is these regulations that are of particular concern to identity changers.

WHY IS THIS IMPORTANT?

Typically, books on the subject of identity changing fail to establish the importance of the SSN as an identifier and its impact on the privacy of the individual. In fact, some books actually insist that the SSN is not an identifier. Though it may be true that the SSN was not designed as a general identifier (I have my doubts), it is certainly erroneous to state that it has not become one.

I've read suggestions to "make up" a SSN and that the SSN is "no big deal." Prior to the 1980s, there may have been some truth to these claims. However, with government's increasing desire to reduce acts of fraud, the identity changer will certainly want to keep the following laws in mind:

A 1981 amendment to Section 208(g) of the Social Security Act makes it a criminal offense to:

- Alter, buy, sell, or counterfeit a Social Security card
- Possess a genuine or counterfeit Social Security card with intent to sell or alter it

Additionally, violations of Section 208 were changed from misdemeanors to felonies by the following provision:

- All violations of Section 208 of the Social Security Act committed after December 29, 1981, are felonies with penalties of up to $5,000 fine, up to 5 years in jail, or both.

In 1982 the False Identification Crime Control Act added Section 1028 to Title 18 of the United States Code, which provides for penalties of "not more than $25,000 or imprisonment for not more than 5 years, or both" for particular offenses involving false identification documents. The section clearly defines an identification document as "any document commonly accepted for the purpose of identification of individuals." Therefore, Social Security cards would be included under this Section. See Appendix D for the entire text of Section 1028.

Even as early as 1976, the Tax Reform Act amended Section 208(g) of the Social Security Act, making it a federal criminal offense to misuse a SSN for any reason. Prior to that, only issues of fraud against the SSA were addressed.

In addition to the above laws and potential penalties for misuse of the SSN, there are other significant reasons why the identity changer will want to take care in choosing a number.

Using the Social Security Death Index (SSDI), credit reporting agencies cross-reference SSNs of deceased individuals with their existing credit profiles. If the SSN you invent happens to belong to a deceased person, there is a good chance your credit report will be flagged for potential fraud. Believe me, you don't need this kind of flag in your new life.

Care must also be taken when establishing a bank account with an acquired SSN. Banks may receive bulletins from the Social Security Administration that indicate the most recently issued SSNs. A 50-year-old man who walks into a bank with a SSN issued last quarter, or not yet issued, would be suspect.

Also, the IRS sends out a watch list of fraudulent SSNs to banks and other entities. The banks are supposed to search for accounts and safe deposit boxes connected with the SSNs on this circular.

After reading the above laws, regulations, and policies, it should be obvious that great care is needed in inventing, choosing, and using a Social Security Number.

CONSTRUCTION OF THE SSN

Some books on the subject of identity changing do explain the significance of the first three digits of the SSN. Unfortunately, the explanation stops there and is very limited even at that. Here is a detailed explanation of the entire SSN.

The SSN is a nine-digit number separated by two dashes into three segments. The first segment is comprised of three digits and, with the exception of the 700 series, indicates the area of the country in which the number was issued. (The 700 series was reserved for railroad retirement use.) This segment is referred to as the "area" segment. The middle segment is composed of two digits and is used to break the numbers from each area into groups. This segment is known as the "group" or "block" segment. The last segment is composed of four digits and is used to serialize about 10,000 numbers (0001 through 9999) within each group. This is called the "serial" or "serial number" segment. Thus we have:

AREA—BLOCK—SERIAL NUMBER
arranged as:
aaa-bb-ssss
where a = area, b = block, and s = serial number

When dealing with bureaucrats, it is important for the identity changer to understand the significance of each segment of the SSN.

The area segment of the SSN indicates to the bureaucrat where the number was issued. If an uninformed identity changer invents a SSN beginning with 035, a savvy bureaucrat may know that this number should have been issued in the state of Rhode Island. The particularly cunning bureaucrat may make light conversation with the identity changer, inquiring as to where he grew up and places he may have lived. If the uninformed identity changer gets caught up in this phony conversation and unwittingly admits that he's never been in Rhode Island, the bureaucrat will become very suspicious. By the same token, if the identity changer invents a SSN that should have been issued in Alabama, yet he speaks with a strong Long Island accent, this may also raise suspicions in the savvy bureaucrat. When inventing a Social Security Number, you will want to use the area listings found in Appendix A while keeping the above caveats in mind.

With a little planning, it is a relatively simple task to obtain or invent a SSN that contains the proper first three digits needed for your intended purposes (i.e., where your new identity claims to be from). Choosing or finding a SSN with the appropriate block segment is somewhat more involved.

In many of the books I've read on this subject, the middle two digits of the SSN are often said to be unimportant. This is simply not the case. These digits give bureaucrats an idea of when the number was issued. In fact, look at a copy of your credit report sometime. You will find a line that states, "The Social Security Number you gave us was issued between 1956 and 1958" (the actual years may vary). What would be the point of inventing a credit profile that has your birth year as 1964 and your SSN as being issued in 1952? Such a contradiction would flag your report for potential fraud.

That line of your credit report is generated by computer software that compares the middle two digits of your SSN with an in-house database. This type of software and databasing is becoming more and more common. Variations of this software have been implemented as "Project Clean Data" by many state and federal agencies and is used to identify incorrect, unissued, and fraudulently used SSNs.

I have yet to come across a complete, up-to-date listing that details the year of issue for each block segment by state (or area). I have been compiling my own list over the years, albeit somewhat incomplete.

I have learned, and verified through experience, that within each area, odd groupings from 01 through 09 are the first issued. In highly populated states, these groupings were probably issued before 1940. After the 09 block has been used, even numbers from 10 through 98 are issued. Then, as more numbers are needed, even groupings from 02 through 08, then odd groupings from 11 through 99 are issued.

The main thing that the identity changer needs to be concerned with is this: In which year was a particular block of numbers issued in your target area? The book *Social Security Number Fraud* published by Eden Press has a 25-page listing that you may wish to use as a reference. This listing is of poor quality, being photocopies of photocopies of government documents that were probably of poor quality to begin with. Parts of it are all but unreadable. So, for this revised edition of *The Modern Identity Changer*, I have taken the time to redraft this listing into a much more readable Excel spreadsheet. (See Appendix C.)

As long as the block, or middle two digits, of "your" SSN was issued after the year in which you claim to have been born, you have solid ground to stand on when presenting the SSN to bureaucrats.

The Eden SSN listing is only valid from 1951–1978. Some of you may want more information. Knowing this, I have included some guidelines for compiling a SSN database of your own.

Making Your Own Database

The best way to gain a solid understanding of how your state assigns SSNs is to create your own database. To accomplish this, take a notebook and pen with you to the vital statistics office in your state and begin looking through a book of death certificates. To find a recent book, get hold of the most recent index and write down some book numbers from it. Then, find the appropriate book or books.

You will notice that the death certificates indicate the decedent's SSN and age at time of death. These are the two bits of information in which you are primarily interested. Enter the SSN in one column of your notebook and the age the person would be if he or she were still alive, not the age at time of death. This is the reason for using a recent book of death certificates. With a recent book, you will have no need to compensate for the time that has elapsed since the death record was recorded. Many states have a backlog, however, so the most recent book may not yet be available. If this is the case, grab a book that is exactly one year old and simply add one year to all of the given ages on the death certificates.

After you compile a sufficient amount of information, take your notebook home and enter the two columns into a database on your computer. Enter the SSNs in one field and the ages in an adjacent field just as you did in your notebook. It would be interesting to break the SSN into its three component parts and insert these into three separate fields. Then, you can sort the fields by the first three digits, middle two digits, or last four digits to see what kinds of patterns emerge. You are mainly interested in seeing which ages are associated with which middle two digits. The actual year of issue is not all that important for our purposes. We only need a general idea of what SSNs will be valid for the identity we are planning to create.

By the way, if you happen to own a laptop PC, you could create your database right at the vital statistics office and save yourself a step. This is public information, and as long as you don't scan documents into your PC, the bureaucrats should not have a problem with your using a laptop in the research room.

	AREA	BLOCK	AGE	DOD
1	019	52	26	1/1/97
2	014	38	40	1/1/97
3	019	22	65	1/1/97
4	101	26	56	1/1/97
5	110	26	60	1/1/97
6	119	60	20	1/1/97
7	210	56	22	1/1/97
8	224	90	35	1/1/97
9	282	40	83	1/1/97

This method should prove useful to anybody who is willing to take the time to compile the information. My database is compiled from actual credit reports I have reviewed and from credit profiles I have created or helped others to create in my line of work as a private investigator. Obviously, this is the most accurate method. I realize, though, that not everybody is a PI, and that is why I have included the substitute method above.

Another method of determining a SSN's year of issue is to just go ahead and use it in a request for a credit report. When you receive the report, it will tell you the year that the SSN was issued. Then, if the birth date that you used doesn't jibe with the number, simply send in the "Dispute Form" with an amended birth date. The credit bureau will be more than pleased that you have helped them make their files more accurate! Even if it turns out that the SSN is not useful for your specific needs, you will learn something about how the numbers were issued in your state. In this way, you can begin to compile your own database.

Highest Numbers Issued

Banks and other bureaucratic agencies receive quarterly bulletins that show the highest issued SSNs by area. Thus, the middle two digits you choose must not be too high for the area you choose. Appendix B has a listing that was accurate as of November 2002, which should be sufficient for most purposes. However, if it is not, the techniques outlined in the "Making Your Own Database" section above can also be used to determine the highest SSNs issued in your area. Simply make a database of young people with SSNs who have died recently. This will give you a good idea as to the highest block issued in your area.

Updated SSA Information

Since this book's original printing, the SSA has built a Web site worthy of mention. It has pages of useful information, including a complete history of the SSN and some amusing anecdotes. But of paramount importance is that, at least at the time of this writing, the Web site maintains an up-to-date, state-by-state "High Group List" as well as an up-to-date

"Social Security Number Allocations" chart. For some reason the site does not have a geographic and chronological distribution of SSN chart, as appears in Appendix C of this book. Perhaps the information is *too* useful?

Summarizing the Construction of the SSN

Use the above information to make sure that the SSN you invent, borrow, or obtain has the following:

- Valid area number that supports the claims of your new identity
- Valid block number that was not issued prior to the date on which you claim to have been born
- Valid block number that is not higher than the highest number issued for the area segment of the SSN you are borrowing or inventing
- Valid serial number (not 0000)

APPLYING FOR A SSN

The other option for obtaining a SSN is to actually apply for one under your new identity. This method offers several advantages if you are intending to disappear for good. If you use this method, you will have fewer hassles gaining and maintaining employment under your new identity. Also, when you retire you can collect Social Security benefits, providing the program is still in existence.

The problem with this method is that most identity changers are too old to be applying for a SSN. Though one is never legally too old to apply for a SSN, most folks have obtained one by the time they are 15 years old. So, a 30-year-old man applying for a new SSN would appear conspicuous.

At the time of this writing, the SSA appears to have an internal policy of verifying birth certificates for all applicants over 17 years of age. This means you cannot use a counterfeit birth certificate for a new identity over the age of 17. If you try to do so, your application will be delayed and you will receive a letter in the mail within a few weeks stating that your birth certificate does not match the SSA's data. Of course there are ways around this quandary.

There are two tricks I'll present. Both methods involve applying as an individual under age 18. Why would you do that if you are in fact much older? Because the Social Security card will not state your age anyway; it will only state your name and SSN. Besides, you seldom have to show anybody the card; you usually just tell them your SSN when they ask for it. So an SSN obtained using the methods below is just as good as any "legitimate" SSN. For example, the bank you deal with will not care why an apparently 50-year-old man has a recently issued SSN. In most cases they won't even know it's recently issued, and even if they did know, they wouldn't care. They might assume you were disabled or imprisoned or any number of things. Bottom line: If your SSN satisfies their "High Group Listing," they won't even blink.

Trick #1

If the person applying for a SSN is under 18 years of age, application may be made via U.S. mail. The Social Security Administration requires that you submit original documents or certified copies of the following:

- Your birth certificate
- Some form of identity, such as a driver's license, school record, medical record, or any of the following: U.S. government or state employee ID card; passport; school ID card, record, or report card

You can either forge your own birth certificate in any name you'd like, or, using the methods outlined above in the section on birth certificates, you can adopt the BC of a person who:

- Died very young
- Did not have a SSN
- Would be 16–17 years old today

Now you have a valid birth certificate meeting the first requirement of the SSA. The next logical step is to create a secondary ID that is acceptable to the SSA. The safest choice is a school ID card. They are easy to create and are not standardized. Use the methods in Chapter 6 to create a school ID card that contains the following information:

- Name of school. Be sure to use a real school that is located in the town where you claim to reside (i.e., where your mail drop is).
- "Your" name.
- Student ID number.
- YOG. This is the year of graduation, which all bureaucrats abbreviate YOG. Use a YOG that is the same year in which you are applying for the SSN. This will make it look consistent with the ruse that we will use below.
- Photo. Be sure to use the photograph of a high school student here. If you happen to have someone's old high school ID (not your own), you can use the photo from that. If not, you will need to find another source such as a high school yearbook. Or hire a teenager for some job and tell him he must bring two passport photos for his work ID. Use one for his work ID and the other one for "your" high school ID. A nice touch on a high school ID is to add some trivial information to the back of it, such as homeroom number, bus shift, school address and hours, etc. Of course, if you have some other form of secondary ID to offer the SSA, by all means use it!

You are now going to write to the SSA and submit your identity documents. Use a piece of yellow lined paper and a cheap blue pen to write your note. If the pen happens to be a little leaky, that helps too. You are trying to create the image that you are, indeed, a high school student.

In your note to the SSA, state that you are in need of a SSN because your parents told you to get a job, or you need a job so that you can buy a car, go to the prom, pay for college, or whatever. Just make it sound like a teen is writing the letter. Tell the SSA that you have "sent them the documents that they told you to send" or similar teenage wording. Do not begin the letter, "Enclosed please find the documents necessary to facilitate issuing . . ." This would give you away as an experienced letter writer, which most high school students are not.

What I'm about to tell you to do may seem strange. In fact, it may seem like suicide. In your letter to the SSA, include the address of the school "in case you have any questions." It may also help to include the phone number and the name of a guidance counselor at the school.

What? What if they call? I hear your panic. The idea is to make the application look as legitimate as possible. A teenager is not used to dealing with bureaucracies and would want the SSA to call the school if there are any problems. But of course, you know there are no problems with the application. The only potential problem is that the SSA bureaucrat may be suspicious of fraud, right? Well, when you include the school address and phone number, the lazy bureaucrat will think, "Hey, who would give me the school address and phone number if they were trying to commit fraud?" Hopefully, the bureaucrat will OK your application and go to lunch.

When you are done composing your letter, send it to the SSA field office in your state capital. Do not use a field office local to the school you are claiming to attend, as the bureaucrats there may be familiar with the school and/or its IDs. Also, don't just send your application to a field office on the other side of the state. It would look suspicious if you sent your application to anywhere but your local field office or the state capital. The office at the capital expects to get mail from all over the state, whereas local field offices expect only local mail.

The best time to apply is late spring to early summer when the SSA is busy filling many requests similar to yours. One caveat for the not-so-brazen: be aware of the possibility that a savvy SSA bureaucrat may have already processed SSN applications from the same school. If that applicant also used his or her school ID to apply, the bureaucrat may wonder why your ID looks different. If possible, get a peek at a legitimate ID prior to creating yours.

Trick #2

If you are very young, say 18–21, you can go into the SSA office as "yourself" and apply for an SSN using a forged birth certificate and simply lying about your age, saying you are 17. Otherwise, you will have to go into the office as your parent.

Example: 32-year-old Jim Smith has a state ID he obtained by supplying a well-crafted birth certificate to his friendly Bureau of Motor Vehicles bureaucrat. Some states, such as Texas, need nothing more than this. You can get a state ID in other states, such as Massachusetts, by having an accomplice swear on the holy holy that you are Jim Smith and supplying any old lame piece of ID such as an electric bill.

So Mr. Smith has a state ID card. Now he needs an SSN in the same name. Mr. Smith is already good with birth certificates so he makes another one for James Smith, Jr., who was born a couple years back. Mr. Smith also crafts some other documents, such as a vaccination record and a baptismal certificate. He goes to a busy SSA field office and applies for his son's SSN. He will need his own birth certificate and state-issued ID as proof of his paternity.

Once the application is completed in the field office, it will take three to four weeks to receive the SSN via mail.

Covering Your Bases

The above scenarios should work most of the time. The other side of the coin is that the bureaucrat may call the school (if using Trick #1) to see if there really is a Jonathan Derringer, student ID #01234, who attends their school and takes bus number five home to Clarkesville. If this happens, your application will be denied and an investigation may or may not be conducted.

If you suspect that this has happened, abandon your address and start the process over again.

Under no circumstances should you use the same address for more than 10 SSNs. Under the SSA's "Project Map," if more than 10 Social Security cards are mailed to the same address, a computer at the SSA will flag that address for potential fraud. Modern identity changers use one address for each application.

Here's an interesting fact that might help you backstop a new identity, especially if you're an older identity changer. Identity changers know that it can be hard to backstop a made-up identity with a high school education. Usually, you have to go through old yearbooks and borrow someone else's education. But if you can find a school system that destroys their old records, nobody can prove or disprove that you attended that school system.

I recently tried to get the school records of a 36-year-old client from his hometown, only to find out that they'd all been transferred to the regional vocational high school he'd attended in another town. I called the high school. They confirmed that the client's entire file from kindergarten through high school had been archived there for almost 20 years. They then told me that all records 15 years or older had been slated for destruction. As is typical with such bureaucratic decisions, some records, though such slated, had not yet been destroyed. I had the woman search the archive for my client's records. She called back the next day saying there were no records whatsoever since all the ones from his year of graduation had indeed been destroyed. I asked, "So this man tells me he went to your school and I have no way to prove this?" She told me that I was correct.

So anybody 30 years or older could say they attended this vocational school, and other bureaucrats would have no way to verify or disprove it. With some homemade documents, an identity changer could create a complete educational history with IQ test scores and transcripts. Those with the proper resources could even have a special yearbook printed up, or a black and white picture laser-printed in the blank space right after Lenny Zwigmyer's face.

Finding this type of situation can actually be better than backstopping an ID. Since Big Brother is at fault for destroying the records, he will all the more quickly turn a blind eye to the matter. This situation may arise more frequently these days due to local budget cuts. Schools can't maintain old records because the fed is forking over less aid money. So you see, Big Brother occasionally bites himself in the ass! You just have to be aware when he does so in order to take advantage.

POCKETBOOK SSNs [1]

The most misused SSN of all time was 078-05-1120. In 1938 the E.H. Ferree wallet manufacturing company in Lockport, New York, decided to promote its product by showing how a Social Security card would fit into its wallets. A sample card, used for display purposes, was inserted in each wallet. Company vice president and treasurer Douglas Patterson thought it would be a clever idea to use the actual SSN of his secretary, Mrs. Hilda Schrader Whitcher.

The wallet was sold by Woolworth stores and other department stores all over the country. Even though the card was only half the size of a real card, was printed all in red, and had the word "specimen" written across the face, many purchasers of the wallet adopted the SSN as their own. In the peak year of 1943, 5,755 people were using Hilda's number. The SSA acted to eliminate the problem by voiding the number and publicizing that it was incorrect to use it. Mrs. Whitcher was, of course, given a new number. However, the number continued to be used for many years. In all, more than 40,000 people reported this as their SSN. As late as 1977, 12 people were found to still be using the SSN "issued by Woolworth."

Mrs. Whitcher recalled coming back from lunch one day to find her fellow workers teasing her about her newfound fame. They were singing the refrain from a popular song of the day: *Here comes the million-dollar baby from the five and ten cent store.*

Although the snafu gave her a measure of fame, it was mostly a nuisance. The FBI even showed up at her door to ask her about the widespread use of her number. In later years she observed: "They started using the number. They thought it was their own. I can't understand how people can be so stupid. I can't understand that."

The New York wallet manufacturer was not the only one to cause confusion about SSNs. More than a dozen similar cases have occurred over the years—usually when someone publishes a facsimile of an SSN using a made-up number. The Whitcher case, however, is far and away the worst involving a real SSN and an actual person.

One embarrassing episode was the fault of the Social Security Board itself. In 1940 the board published a pamphlet explaining the new program and showing a facsimile of a card on the cover. The card in the illustration used a made-up number of 219-09-9999. Sure enough, in 1962 a woman presented herself to the Provo, Utah, Social Security office complaining that her new employer was refusing to accept her old Social Security Number—219-09-9999. When it was explained that this could not possibly be her number, she whipped out her copy of the 1940 pamphlet to prove that yes indeed it was her number!

Because of this phenomenon, there are currently well over 200 documented "pocketbook" Social Security Numbers, each caused by some organization displaying an actual number in its advertising. I have included here for your pleasure a list of some of the more popular pocketbook numbers. These numbers exist, they are no longer in use, and they can come in handy in a pinch. Memorizing even a few or even one of these numbers can get you past that annoying SSN: ___-__-____

line on just about any bureaucratic form that you fill out. Does a video store really need to know your true SSN, especially when they also have your credit card number on file? What about the dentist or your Internet Service Provider? Whenever some snot-nosed low-level bureaucrat insists you must provide an SSN, simply rattle off one you've memorized from the below listing.

078-05-1120 (Hilda S. Whitcher's original number!)
219-09-9999 (The one from the SSA pamphlet.)
022-28-1852
141-18-5941
212-09-7694
042-10-3580
165-15-7999
062-36-0749
155-18-7999
306-30-2348
165-20-7999
308-12-5070
095-07-3645
165-22-7999
468-28-8779
128-03-6045
165-24-7999
549-24-1889
135-01-6629
189-09-2294
937-65-4320

Before we move on to the finer points of establishing residence, gaining education, and setting up business entities, I'd like to leave you with the following.

The above information pertaining to birth certificates and Social Security Numbers varies greatly by state and is constantly changing. Always bear in mind that there is a constant need for updated solutions to the identity problem. So stay on top of your research. Verify all "facts" you dig up on these topics, especially ones gleaned from the Internet. Be especially careful to catalog counties that cross-check birth and death records. Be aware of reciprocal agreements between states that may have developed similar cross-checking schemes.

ENDNOTE

1. Woolworth–Whitcher anecdote reprinted from the SSA Web site.

CHAPTER FOUR

Establishing Residence

～•

Leaving home in a sense involves a kind of second birth
in which we give birth to ourselves.
—Robert Neelly Bellah

"Where do you live?"

How do you answer such a question? Most people automatically interpret this question as, "Where is your home?" If a police officer asks you where you live, you understand that he or she is trying to find out where you make your home. This latter interpretation is really not all that much clearer a question, but because we as a society agree on its meaning, we generally respond by telling people where we typically eat, sleep, and entertain guests. We do this, usually, by giving a location derived from incremental subdivisions of the earth's surface.

For example, we might tell the officer, "Boulder, Colorado." Colorado is already understood to be a subdivision of a landmass we've all agreed to call the United States. The officer further understands Boulder to be a subdivision of the land area known as Colorado. Being a bureaucrat, and therefore an information hound, the officer would likely insist that you further descry our otherwise whimsical and free-forming universe down to a specific point known as a street address. Failure to do so would land you at another specific point known as a jail cell—this latter possibility resulting from the officer's liberal interpretation of the local vagrancy laws, or simply because he feels like arresting you.

Now I pose the question to you as a philosopher: "Where

do you live?" If you think a minute, you might interpret the question to mean, "Where do you exist?" or "Where is your consciousness centered?" Well, you live wherever you're at. In a truly free society, nobody ever needs to know any more than that. Remember the contrasting definitions of identity from Chapter 1? That's what we're dealing with here. But tell the officer that you live wherever you are and see how far that gets you. So, as also mentioned in Chapter 1, we are forced to provide Big Brother with his little papers and details. This chapter explores some ways of doing that as far as residence is concerned. Since bureaucrats usually want a way to get hold of you while you are at your residence, I've also included a section on dealing with society's apparent necessity for telephone communication.

PART ONE: ADDRESS

If you've ever been down and out, you know the importance of having an address. You can't send your kids to school without one. You can't apply for government assistance without one. Politicians talk about feeding the homeless, but bureaucrats can't give out food stamps unless the homeless person has an address. Er, excuse me Mr. Politician, have you seriously considered the word *homeless*? It means you have no address! A street address, whether or not associated with an actual building, renders the impression that you have a home or, more important to the bureaucrat, a place where you can be found, contacted, taxed, policed, harassed, and generally accessible to Big Brother. Sounds like fun, right? So let us explore how to keep our information-hungry friends happy . . . .

MAIL DROPS

Days before this book's original release in September of 1997, the United States Postal Service published in the Federal Register a proposed rule to amend sections of its Domestic

Mail Manual. The proposed rule was to revise its policies regarding delivery of mail to "Commercial Mail Receiving Agencies," or CMRAs. CMRAs are colloquially known as mail drops. A mail drop is an establishment that rents mailbox space much like the U.S. Post Office rents post office boxes.

There used to be two advantages typical to mail drop establishments. One advantage was that the mail drop facility allowed its "tenants" to use its full street address, such as 1313 Mockingbird Lane, and then add the mailbox number as a suite number. This yielded an address that looked like:

>   Mr. Frank N. Stein
>   1313 Mockingbird Lane, Suite 39
>   Transylvania, PA 12345

The middle line of this address looked much more "established" than if it read P.O. Box 1313. The U.S. Postal Service does not allow its box holders this advantage. Because of this established look, many entrepreneurs employed the services of mail drops for purposes of appearing, well, established.

Often, picking up the mail on a daily basis becomes inconvenient. This brings us to the second advantage of using a mail drop establishment: mail forwarding. Mail drops still have this advantage. Many drops, for an additional service charge, will package up your mail on a weekly basis and forward it to you at your "real" address. This address could be another mail drop if you happen to be an especially private person or are simply of the more paranoid sort. You decide how much anonymity you want. It may best suit your needs to pick up your own mail and eliminate any paper trail. Some mail drops have 24-hour access, and these are recommended if you'd rather not be on a first-name basis with the hired help. Got it?

Now for the bad news. Some people used mail drops for fraudulent purposes, and this was the Postal Service's stated reason for proposing rule changes regarding CMRAs. The

• ✒

most significant and controversial of the proposed new rules was that of requiring CMRA mailboxes to be designated as private mailboxes by use of the prefix "PMB" (for "private mailbox") as opposed to "suite" or "apartment" or anything else for that matter. Any mail sent to a CMRA mailbox not so designated would be returned to sender marked "Undeliverable as addressed."

I wish to point out here that the U.S. Postal Service—a supposedly privatized organization in direct competition with CMRAs—is somehow allowed to create a rule that would adversely affect its competition. If any other private organization on the face of the planet had so egregiously attempted to influence competition in a manner even half as blatant as the Postal Service did, the Justice Department would have slapped it with antitrust suits in short order.

The proposed rule changes naturally sparked a war between CMRAs such as Mailboxes Etc. and the U.S. Postal Service. Law enforcement, government, and most bureaucrats sided with the U.S. Postal Service. Privacy organizations, homeless shelters, and battered women's groups sided with the CMRAs. The battle waged for years, with various compromises brought to the table, all of which were shot down by the USPS.

The question was put out for public comment early on. The overwhelming majority of the comments opposed the new rules. Only 10 of the 8,107 comments received by the USPS supported the rule changes. Let me just show you that as a percentage before we go on: one one-thousandth of one percent (.001%) in favor. That's 99.999 percent opposed, my friends.

What do you think happened?

The question was put out to public comment ostensibly so the USPS would consider public opinion before deciding whether to change the rules. With 99.999 percent of the public *opposed* . . .

[drum roll please]

. . . the law *passed*.

The lesson? As a citizen of the United States of America, your comments and opinions mean absolutely nothing to your government. Can you say *Jack shit*?

So who supported the proposed rule changes besides the USPS and law enforcement officials? Large firms and associations, including financial institutions and trade associations of mailers. The next lesson? If you're a big corporation with a lot of money, your comments and opinions mean a lot to the government. And the government wonders why people would want to hide from it!

So how does a modern identity changer establish a virtual residence under these new rules? Well, one solution is to just go ahead and use mail drops. Many people still don't understand what the PMB designation means anyway. This is especially true if you pretend to be from a rural or unincorporated area. People expect to see all sorts of weird addressing schemes when they write to someone living in the boonies.

You can also add some other designators of your own to make the PMB stand out less. For example:

Jane Smith
c/o PMB Corp.
1200 Main Street, PMB 12
Deliverance, USA

John Doe
FMS Subd., #14
128 Elm Street, PMB 14
Deliverance, USA

Chris Pat
RR16
128 Elm Street, PMB 16
Deliverance, USA

Obviously you'd have to use care in choosing your mail drop. If you want your address to sound residential, avoid business-sounding roads such as Main Street, Kings Highway, or Avenue of the Americas.

But wait, Obi Wan, there is another hope . . . .

Office Business Centers

Office business centers (OBCs) that follow strict guidelines are exempt from CMRA regulations. An office business center is a shared office space where entrepreneurs share things like conference rooms, computers, copiers, secretarial services, and telephone answering services. One can readily see the temptation to pay an OBC a few dollars to act as a mail drop. Unfortunately, the USPS also readily saw this temptation and enacted the following rules that OBCs must follow to avoid being classified as CMRAs. The OBC must:

- Have a very specific written contract with each of its customers
- Obligate the customer to a minimum of 16 hours of part-time office usage at market rates
- Offer full-time receptionist services
- Offer full-time "live personal" telephone answering service
- List each client on the building directory
- Allow each client access to conference rooms and other business services on demand
- Maintain contract in force for every single customer

Obviously the OBC has to jump through innumerable hoops to keep the USPS happy. I'd considered italicizing all the unreasonable demands but realized there'd be more italics than not. The fact that they cannot sell anybody less than 16 hours of service, for example, hurts many young entrepreneurs. I wonder how many would-be upstarts never up and start because they can't afford the minimum contract? This is yet another way the government squelches our progress as a nation.

The good news is that OBCs are available for your use, and there are a few that have managed to stay off the CMRA list. It's an open question as to what "market rates" are, so one can readily see that these centers, especially new and hungry ones, can be used as mail drops at least until the USPS takes them to court for failure to comply with its regulations. Then the OBC can simply open its doors under a new name, and the USPS will have to take them to court all over again. Maybe you'll start your own OBC that offers a very competitive rate for 16 hours of service. Maybe you'll start a nonprofit OBC with a government grant, one that gives an advantage to a disadvantaged segment of our society. Then the USPS will have to get off its ass and draft all sorts of new regulations to keep you from acting as a mail drop for your customers. This would keep Big Brother busy for a while and also create some bad PR for him. Of course he'll eventually win and continue to squelch and dumb down his own society, but keeping him busy with current laws will slow his progress inventing new ones.

Option number two is to simply fork over the market rate to the OBC and you'll have your mail drop.

So, mail drops are still available, folks. Just be prepared to pay for them.

Or not . . . .

Make Your Own Mail Drop

Before moving on, I'd like to mention that the whole CMRA–OBC debate is being monitored by the excellent group Postalwatch.org, which can be found online at www.postalwatch.org. Keep an eye on that Web page to see when cheap mail drops may again become available. They also track a host of holy horrors pertaining to the so-called privatized postal service, which for some strange reason seems to operate in lockstep with the whim of the federal government.

But until a winged pig swoops down and nips at your eyebrow or you freeze off your little pinky toes during a day trip to hell, you will probably have to create cheap mail drops of your own. Here are two ideas to get your creative juices flowing.

The condominium where I live has outside mailboxes for each unit. You've seen them—they are the big aluminum cubes that contain 16 mailboxes each. My building happens to have 30 units, which requires two cubes, or 32 mailboxes. Gee, there just happens to be two leftover boxes. One is used for outgoing mail. Would you like to take a guess as to who uses the other one?

It's amazing the impression a clipboard and tie can make on a mailman. "Hi, I'm from ABC Property Management, and the new tenant in number 32 has been on my ass for a key."

"32?" asks the confused mailman.

"Yeah, used to be for storage only. Probably why there's no spare mailbox key in the office. The association finally decided to rent it out."

"Hmmm. Whatever."

"I brought an aftermarket lock set. Would you mind popping the box for me?"

By the way, the clipboard that says ABC Property Management is just another form of ID.

Granted, it would probably be a bad idea to invent an entire condominium unit on the route of a veteran mail carrier. If the carrier has had the route for any length of time, he may become suspicious of the new unit box. But, if you know of a mail carrier who happens to be retiring soon, you may want to check out his route to see which condominiums he delivers to. Overwhelmed and anxious to learn the route, the new delivery person won't blink twice when delivering mail to unit number 31!

Know of any vacant lots or abandoned buildings? While the post office usually won't deliver to these addresses, you can still use them for some purposes. Use the address as your residence, but file a mail forwarding card with the post office. Have the mail delivered wherever you like, depending on your needs. Anybody can file a mail forwarding card—you do not have to prove prior residence, nor do you have to file the card in person. It can all be done—you guessed it—through the mail! Just keep in mind you'll have to refile the forwarding order when it expires if you need the service for more than a year.

The U.S. Post Office as a Mail Drop

I have a good friend who is one of the freest spirits I know. She does things that most people only dream about. She has hiked the Appalachian Trail and the Cascadia Mountain Range. When she goes on a backcountry trip with a planned route, she leaves her itinerary with me. With a small amount of research, we are able to determine small towns she'll be passing through on her journey. Together, we pick some strategically located towns so she can hop off trail to grab a shower and an occasional decent night's sleep at a cheap motel. But I wouldn't let my good friend spend the night in a strange town without some good cheer and a care package from home. So what to do?

It's called General Delivery and, though it's supposedly reserved for rural areas without local carriers, I've yet to find a post office that will refuse to provide me this service, anytime or anyplace.

Let's say my friend's name is Lisa Lisa. I package up some handwritten letters of life back home, some nonperishable food items, a stuffed animal to keep her company, and certain pagan artifacts depending on the projected moon phase on her arrival date in Deliverance, USA. Since there are no perishable items, I can send the package weeks in advance of her projected arrival and be sure it will be at the post office when she gets to Deliverance. I simply address it:

> Lisa Lisa
> c/o General Delivery
> Deliverance, USA BCDBC-ABGA

The Deliverance post office will hold the package for up to 30 days. Lisa would only need to present "proper identification" to claim the package (though in practice, Lisa has told me identification isn't even requested half the time). Other than my cost of mailing the package, there is no fee for this service. The USPS states explicitly that this is a good service "for transients or those with no permanent address." So the very entity that enacted such strict rules for CMRAs[1] has left its own policies very liberal.

ESTABLISHING ACTUAL RESIDENCE

If you've decided that you're opting out of this mess altogether and starting a new life under a new identity, you will want to establish an actual residence as opposed to just a mail drop. The identity documents you obtain will determine if you can buy a home under your new identity. For instance, if you do not yet have a valid driver's license under your new identity, you are probably not ready to purchase a home through the usual channels of real estate acquisition.

When buying a home through the usual channels, there are lawyers and real estate agents involved. These people may ask you for identity-verifying documents or information at various stages of the transaction. However, the only point of a real estate transaction where there will be a legitimate need for actual identity documents will be at the closing. The attorneys will want to have notarized signatures from both the buyer and seller. Practically speaking, it is more important that the signature of the seller be notarized than the signature of the buyer. The buyer's attorney wants to be sure that the person collecting thousands of dollars from his client is indeed the true owner of the property. As the typical real estate transaction involves a mortgage, the buyer has bank documents to sign and the bank will expect a notarized signature on at least the mortgage deed. The usual identity document requested for notarization is a driver's license.

Remember, the above rules hold true if you intend to go through the usual channels for buying property. But there are several ways to buy property. Keep in mind that neither an attorney nor a real estate agent is necessary to complete a real estate transaction. In fact, many states don't even require a notarized signature on the deed, nor is title to a property necessarily invalid if it is not filed with the county. In these states, such formalities are still considered preventative measures. The courts do not want ordinary people to lose their property for failure to comply with certain technicalities. Check your state's applicable laws.

Property Purchasing Alternatives

The biggest point an anonymous buyer needs to remember is this: In most states, you can receive title to real property without ever lifting a pen. If you don't need a mortgage, you don't have to sign anything, nor do you have to produce any ID.

Here is a typical scenario where a buyer would not have to sign a thing.

1. Buyer does not use a Realtor.
2. Buyer finds property for sale by owner.
3. Buyer makes a verbal offer and seller accepts.
4. Buyer sets date, time, and place of closing.
5. Seller shows up with attorney.
6. Buyer gives Seller cash or bank check.
7. Seller's attorney shows Seller where to sign the deed.
8. Seller's attorney notarizes Seller's signature.
9. Seller's attorney hands deed to Buyer.
10. Buyer records the deed (or not) at county deeds registry.

Now, let's analyze this transaction step-by-step.

Buyer does not use a Realtor. This step is straightforward. Don't retain the services of a buyer's agent. Don't respond to ads that list properties through real estate agents.

• ⤳

Buyer finds property for sale by owner. Go out and look for "For Sale by Owner" signs, or look in newspaper classifieds for people selling property on their own. There're more than you might think.

Buyer makes a verbal offer and seller accepts. Real estate agents might claim that this is illegal and violates various state "Statutes of Frauds." Neither is true. In order for this contract to be enforceable, it must be in writing. It is still a legal oral contract; you just couldn't enforce it in court if one of the parties backs out.

Buyer sets date, time, and place of closing. Basically, you say, "I'll be at the Suffolk County Deeds Registry (or wherever) at 10:00 A.M. on Monday the 16th." You hope the Seller shows up.

Seller shows up with attorney. Good. Seller is ready to play.

Buyer gives Seller cash or bank check. In reality, you don't usually hand over the check first, but it's a good idea to have your payment plainly visible, especially given the informal nature of the transaction. It will put the Seller and his attorney at ease.

Seller's attorney shows Seller where to sign the deed. With no mortgage, note, or title insurance documents to fill out, this is the next step.

Seller's attorney notarizes Seller's signature. A real estate attorney will usually be able to notarize documents. Attorneys are considered extensions of the court system and, as such, the court sees no conflict of interest when an attorney notarizes his own client's signature. This is common practice.

Seller's attorney hands deed to Buyer. Congratulations! Now you, the Seller, and his attorney know that you own the property.

Buyer records the deed (or not) at county deeds registry. If you want the rest of the world to know you own the property, then you record the deed. If you have some reason why you'd rather not have your name in searchable databases, most states don't require a deed to be recorded. Just pay your property taxes in advance, and the previous owner won't get a tax bill. If he does, it will reflect the account as "Paid in Full" and he won't worry about it.

An unrecorded deed is valid between all parties that have "actual notice" of the property transaction, meaning anybody who sat at the closing table. So don't worry that the Seller can reclaim title to the property if you don't record the deed. You'd have the actual deed (hopefully in a fire safe or something). I presently have four unrecorded deeds in my safe and one unrecorded mortgage discharge. I can record them whenever I want.

For example—worst-case scenario—the Seller goes to land court and files a suit to reclaim "his" property. I'm telling you this will never happen, but let's explore this just for argument's sake. You show up at the court hearing with the deed to your property. The judge asks the Seller why his notarized signature is on the deed if he did not sell you the property.

If this ever did happen, it would be because a greedy and ignorant Seller somehow found out the deed had not been recorded, probably from his half-wit friend who just started taking real estate classes and thinks he's all hip. So they hatch a scheme . . . whatever. Come land court day, the Seller may say, "Well, the deed was never recorded."

The judge would say that doesn't matter—the Seller had actual notice of the transaction—and dismiss the case. You could even win a cross-complaint against the Seller for his malice and willful negligence—compensatory by exemplary or so-called punitive damages.

What? You haven't enough money to buy a house with cash? Don't fret. There are other alternatives.

Buy Raw Acreage and Improve It

Raw acreage is cheap in rural areas. Often it's so cheap you can get into a parcel with your bank account savings or a cash advance from your favorite credit card company. I know people who've won raw acreage in poker games. A friend of

• ➤

mine accepted raw acreage from another acquaintance as payment in full on a defaulted debt.

Raw acreage is often owned by people out-of-state who thought they might like to go hunting or whatever once in a while. After a few eight-hour drives to "the land," they decide it's no longer worth the bother. There are hundreds of other scenarios. Point being, many out-of-state owners of raw acreage in rural areas are anxious to sell it. As such, they are willing to accept creative financing arrangements. Often they are so anxious to recover their lost capital, they will take payment in the form of a 100 percent financed note. Some people won't even retain an attorney because only a few thousand dollars are involved. They may use a preprinted legal form to make the deal with you. Even a hastily scrawled note on a napkin is legal, and you will own the land for as long as you make the payments.

Developer Financing

If you have a driver's license or enough ID to satisfy a notary, you can often purchase improved land through developers willing to finance it to you. There are developers who find land, subdivide it, survey it, conduct site and water percolation tests, and generally prep the land for buyers ready to build houses. They handle all the bureaucracy with the townspeople and sell off the lots for profit.

Often, these developers will sell off the lots with 10 percent down, though they will charge 2 to 4 percent above market interest rates on the note. They will have a credit form for you to fill out, but it is unlikely they will check your information against a credit bureau. Even if they do and the credit bureau returns "No File Found," they won't care. The payments are so small on these loans, they know almost anybody can make them. And if you don't make the payments, they have it written into the mortgage deed that they can foreclose on you within 30 days.

Now, you will need to sign something and have it notarized. You will need to sign the mortgage deed back to the developer. This is usually done very informally at his attorney's office, and the developer may not even be there. All you'll need is a decent-looking driver's license to get through the notary process and you'll have your land.

Real Estate Closings by Mail

Often, the informal transactions related above are done through the mail. This is especially true if you are dealing with an out-of-state seller. This offers a certain opportunity for undocumented citizens in need of a notarized signature. The seller or his attorney will forward you documents through the mail, and you will then have full, private control over them. You can use any number of tricks to get that notary's seal on the document. Chapter 3 of my aforementioned book, *Identity, Privacy, and Personal Freedom: Big Brother vs. The New Resistance*, offers several suggestions. Chapter 5 of my other aforementioned book, *Secrets of a Back-Alley ID Man: Fake ID Construction Techniques of the Underground*, contains several methods to make your own embossing plate or reasonable facsimile thereof. To whet your appetite, I have reproduced one of those methods in Chapter 6 of this book.

Your Humble Abode

So, you've got a little chunk of land. Now what? Most people who manage to get this far probably won't have much money left. If you do, heck, go ahead and build a mansion. If not, you could always just start with a big tent, provided appropriate climate. You can get a cheap two-man pop-up tent for $15 at a discount or surplus store and a sleeping bag for about the same price. You can often find bigger six-man tents at yard sales for not too much money.

If you have a few hundred dollars, you can buy a pop-up trailer. Even if you don't have a car to tow it, an anxious seller might be willing to tow it to your property and help you set it up.

Maybe you plan to build a small cabin. I've done this. If you're used to the city, the woods at night can freak you out more than you might expect. This, to my surprise, happened to me. So, to feel safe until I got used to it, I slept in my truck in a sleep sack. After awhile I realized all those noises at night that sounded like huge animals were nothing more than chipmunks. After gaining more experience in the woods, I learned that you can hear anything big from hundreds of feet away. Pretty soon, all those once-big-sounding crunches and snaps didn't even phase me. I even stopped bringing my rifle with me after awhile.

Before I knew it, I had a first floor built with locking door and window. I set up a cot and had a decent place to sleep. Obviously, you need some carpentry experience to go this route. But that was about all I had. To make sure I was building a sound structure and one that would survive an inspection (even though this town had no building codes, I still wanted to do a good job), I actually bought a book called *Building Your Own House: Everything You Need to Know About Home Construction from Start to Finish* by Robert Roskind (Ten Speed Press, Berkeley, CA, 2000).

One word of advice here, based on my own experience. Don't get too involved with your design. I did, and it's a mistake I'm still paying for. If I had it to do over again, I'd opt for a simple box design with a shed roof. Had I done that, my camp would be finished by now. If you don't know what these terms mean, refer to the above book.

Reading the above, you might be thinking that you have to go to Deliverance, USA, to get good prices on land and to live in a town with no building codes. Actually, my camp is within 25 miles of a major city with all the modern shopping conveniences one could hope for. I am only two miles away from a store that sells all the basic groceries and supplies I might ever need. If your vehicle breaks down, you'll be surprised by how many people will stop and offer their help. People in rural areas know that their survival often depends on others helping them when they are stuck. So in turn, they are eager to help others.

ESTABLISHING A PROFESSIONAL RESIDENCE

By establishing a professional residence such as a law office, doctor's office, or real estate agency, the identity changer effectively kills two birds with one stone. Once a professional residence is established, you will have a residence as well as a business address. It's not illegal for a non-attorney to set up a law office, nor is it illegal for a non-doctor to set up a doctor's office. As long as you don't take on clients or patients or advertise in any way, you are not breaking the law.

Keep a separate business telephone line and your credit applications will look very appealing. In fact, once you become part of a doctor or attorney mailing list, the creditors will seek you out.

You may also wish to maintain a separate business address to make things look even more legitimate. For instance, if you happen to set up your professional residence at 321 Quackery Lane, you may want to use 321 for your office address and R321 for your residential address. The "R" is usually accepted to mean "rear," as in rear of the building. You can think of it as meaning "residence" so that you'll never mix up your addresses. Usually such an address is written as 321R, but if you put the "R" first, the address will look that much more distinct to the credit bureau's computers.

Intimidation Factor

By being known as a professional and behaving in that manner, you will gain instant respect from loan officers, bureaucrats, and almost anybody you meet. It's much easier to pass your new identity off to someone if they're afraid to ask you questions and risk insulting you.

If you are lacking in verbal skills, you may want to brush up on your grammar and word power. Professionals such as doctors and attorneys are typically armed with powerful vocabularies and a professional, well-spoken manner. If you are lacking in either of these areas, people may not believe that you are a professional anything, much less a doctor or lawyer. Once somebody questions this, your whole identity will come into question.

There are several books and tapes dedicated to helping people improve their vocabulary, speaking skills, and memory (memory is linked to vocabulary). Local libraries will either have these materials or be able to direct you to someplace that does. So, did you get your library card yet?

PART TWO: TELEPHONES

A telephone number goes hand-in-hand with an established residence. So much so that, in reality, there are few people who have one without the other. (Anytime a bureaucrat asks for your address, the next question will inevitably be, "telephone number?")

A telephone number billed to your new identity at your new address is very appealing to banks, creditors, employers, and other parties hoping to form business relationships with you. Many lending institutions, including credit card companies, will actually score your credit application a point or two higher if you have a telephone in your own name that is billed to your address of record. (A person who is responsible enough to maintain his own telephone number is deemed more likely to take responsibility for his debts.) A typical point-scoring system for lenders and employers may look like this:

No telephone: 0 points
Telephone in own name: 1 point
Telephone billed to residence: 2 points

The theory is that there are very few people who would go through this amount of trouble to obscure their true identity. Lending institutions are concerned that people who obscure their identity are more apt to skip out on payments or commit an outright fraud.

~ •

ESTABLISHING TELEPHONE SERVICE

If you have an actual residence under a new identity, it is a simple matter to order phone service. In most cases, all you need to tell the phone company is your name, address, and Social Security Number. Be forewarned that the Social Security Number you give may be compared to the Social Security Death Index (SSDI) discussed in Chapter 3. This security check is a recent implementation by some telephone companies.

I once tested this out with Nynex Telecommunications. I called Nynex to order some telephone service for a certain identity. I used the name, address, and SSN of a person whom I knew to be deceased. The entire ordering process went smoothly until the end. The last thing the salesperson asked for was "my" Social Security Number. I gave her the one I knew to be retired and currently residing in the SSDI. The salesperson then placed me on hold, presumably to "get me a number." When she returned she said, "Sorry sir, but I can't give you a number today." When I inquired as to why, she said, "There are no numbers available for your area at the moment." This is an interesting response considering the fact that two entirely new exchanges had opened up in recent years. She suggested that I "call back on Monday." Right.

The point is to keep this example in mind when you are building your new identity. If you want your own phone number and the local phone company has this type of security check, make sure you find yourself a clean SSN!

Voice Mail
Once only available to large companies with big UNIX-based computer systems in the basement, voice mail is now available to any schmuck with a PC, fax/modem/voice card, and the appropriate software. Identity changers can have a different extension associated with different identities. Privacy enthusiasts can turn the tables on telemarketers or bill collectors by giving them a labyrinthine maze of touch-tone options for *them* to deal with.

• ✐

A computer set up in your bedroom might answer the phone in the following manner:

> *Hello. You've reached Flimflam Enterprises. All associates are either away from their desks, on the phone, or busy assisting other customers. If you know your party's extension, you may dial it at any time. If you'd like to leave a message for Zigfreid Flimflam, dial 201. If you'd like to leave a message for Yolanda Flimflam, dial 319. If you'd like a current stock quote, dial 999. To leave a message in the general message area, dial 0 or press *80 to begin sending your fax. Have a nice day.*

Actually, most modern voice mail systems will receive a fax automatically, but if you want to sound big and important . . . well, you get the idea.

Here's another possibility:

> *"Hi, you've reached the home of Mr. Jones. If you're calling regarding a past-due account, please press 9."*

Bill collector presses 9.

> *"Please enter the account number of the past-due account, followed by the pound sign."*

Bill collector grumbles and does this.

> *"Please hold while I look up that account."*

Bill collector waits a good two minutes listening to ads about how to change jobs if you hate being a bill collector. Your computer eventually takes him off hold:

> *"Thank you. Your call has been logged and Mr. Jones will do something about that account as soon as he can. Thank you for calling the residence of Mr. Jones and for using our automated phone answering system."*

Brief pause, followed by a terse:
"Goodbye."

RingMate Lines

A few years back, telephone companies began offering a service whereby more than one phone number can ring at the same line and be billed on the same bill. Each phone number has a distinct ring pattern. The service was originally marketed to households that had teenagers who received lots of calls. The idea is that you can give your teenager his or her own number for their friends to call. When the call comes through for the teen, the parents can identify it by the distinct ring pattern and not be troubled to answer the phone.

It didn't take long for home-based businesses to catch on to this idea. On one bill they could have a home phone, business line, and fax line. The additional RingMate lines usually cost about $3 each as opposed to $30 for a separate service.

The identity changer may wish to keep this wonderful service in mind when setting up a professional residence as described previously in this chapter. Or it might even be helpful when establishing your home residence. Let's say you've just filled out an application to rent an apartment. You could have your present "home" number, where you'd answer in your regular voice. You could then have your current "work" number, where you answer in your professional voice (perhaps with a voice changer) and praise yourself to the landlord checking on your rental application. You could have yet another number where your landlord-to-be can call your "previous landlord," who'll give an equally good recommendation. If you use your noggin, you could dream up other convenient uses for this service.

There are also devices sold by telephone companies and on the open market that will detect the ring pattern of a RingMate line and direct the call to the appropriate device or answering machine. In this way, you can direct your business line to your computer for fax and voice mail services and direct your residential line to an answering machine for a more "homey" greeting.

There is no rule restricting you to only one RingMate line. I know that most phone companies have deals where you can get two RingMate lines for $5. Most ring detectors are also designed to handle more than two rings. So, if you have two businesses, or if you want to give bill collectors a different phone number, or if you want a different phone number for people connected with your past life, you have many options available to you.

Caller ID

A hotly debated privacy issue, but it looks like this one is here to stay. Caller ID is great for identity changers or other folks who may be leery about answering the phone and would like to know who's on the other end before picking up the line.

Another great feature is that you can log all calls placed to your residence even when you're not home. If you see any numbers that look suspicious, you can do reverse number searches through any of several databases available on CD-ROM for a PC. Or, if you don't have a PC (or just like to hate them), you can use a crisscross directory such as those published by Cole Publications. These directories are very expensive, but if you go into any real estate office pretending to be a Realtor from a nearby office, they will usually let you use theirs.

Telephone companies as well as private concerns offer a myriad of Caller ID products for your perusal. If you are being hounded by creditors, a good Caller ID device called The Bouncer is available through Hello Direct. This device allows you to program in certain numbers or area codes that you don't want to deal with. When a person calls from that number or area code, the device "bounces" them out into TelCo limbo. The device will also bounce all calls that have their Caller ID "blocked" if you choose to set this option (blocking Caller ID is a favorite trick of bill collectors and investigators).

Voice Changers

Among the many other goodies available from telephone companies and third parties is the voice changer. A voice changer is a device that can make a man sound like a woman by raising the pitch of his voice or make a woman sound like a man by lowering the pitch. These devices are great for answering the phone in a small business. A man could answer the phone with the voice changer engaged acting as the secretary of the office. When the client on the other end then asks for the big boss, he can place the client on hold, switch the voice changer off, and pick up the phone again in an authoritative manner.

An obvious adaptation of this scheme could be used to avoid bill collectors. If a bill collector is looking for a man, answer the phone as a woman and your act will be all the more convincing.

If a potential employer is calling your "business" to verify past employment, you do not want to answer the phone with the same voice the employer just heard during your interview. Another use of the voice changer is born.

By the way, if you should ever screw up and answer the phone with the voice changer unknowingly disengaged, your client may say, "Gee, you and your boss sound a lot alike." If this happens, without becoming embarrassed or missing a beat, simply state, "You know, everybody tells me that!" and continue about your business.

Answering Services

Answering services are good in a pinch for some business uses, but they are more costly than most other methods, and you never know who is answering the phone for you (e.g., sometimes the employees are incompetent or rude to your callers). Answering services are also a turnoff to many people, and most people know when they've reached one.

For these reasons, employ answering services sparingly and judiciously, if at all.

• ✦

SUMMARY

Much of the information presented in this chapter is linked to or can be used in close conjunction with the ideas to be presented in the next chapter. Residence, telephone service, employment, and education are at the heart of what society considers to be an established identity. By keeping this concept in mind as you read Chapter 5, you will better be able to create that image society is expecting.

ENDNOTE

1. One of the controversial rules is that the CMRA customer must provide a legal mailing address, which battered women's groups strongly opposed since ex-spouses could then track them down easily.

CHAPTER FIVE

Education and Employment

⌣•

For some reason, education and employment always seem to be intertwined. Personally, I've known a lot of MBAs who couldn't run a vacuum cleaner, much less a business. Likewise, I've known a few college slouches who've started bang-up companies. Nevertheless, the system expects that you will be educated in a certain way and that you will then obtain employment based on how many dates you had in college—or something like that.

Regardless of why they are intertwined, you, as an identity changer, will need to know how to obtain education and employment (or reasonable facsimiles thereof).

PART ONE: EDUCATION

From early childhood, we are taught that education is the key to finding a good job, and a good job is the key to providing for a family, and having a family is the key to happiness. Has anybody bothered to look at the latest divorce statistics?

One thing, at least, is true. Employment is often associated with education. In fact, most people's entire lives are centered around these two facets of existence. At an early age we are pushed into the education stream and told that our goal is to acquire sufficient knowledge so that we may eventually obtain a "good job" and have a means to provide for our own survival and perhaps even support a family.

• ⌐

Since these tenets are so ingrained in our society, the identity changer can expect to encounter some special problems relating to them. Some solutions to these problems are presented below.

COLLEGE CREDIT

Instead of attending on-campus classes, there are some really great alternatives to obtaining a college degree. In recent years, a subtle doctrine has begun creeping into our learning institutions. That doctrine is the idea that education takes place in the mind and not in the classroom; that it is the student who is responsible for his or her education and not the institution. Of course, many of the older, larger, and more established institutions of higher education vehemently oppose this radical heresy. Nonetheless, more and more schools are recognizing and granting credit for off-campus study. A good book on this subject is *College Degrees by Mail* by John Bear, published by Ten Speed Press in Berkeley, California.

One of the best legitimate off-campus colleges is Regent's College, which is part of the University of the State of New York and whose central office is located in Albany. There are various ways that credit can be earned at Regent's and similar colleges. A few sources of credit are:

- Transfer of college credits
- College-level proficiency examinations
- Credit by exam
- Advanced placement
- Portfolio-based assessments
- Telecourses
- Correspondence courses
- Independent study
- Community college courses
- Online courses

I mention advanced placement, credit by exam, and proficiency examinations because some of you may have college degrees in one name and would like to have the same degree in another. But if you were one of those people who crammed just to pass the tests and never bothered to remember any of the material, you will find yourself learning it all over again. That said, let's look a bit closer at each of these options.

Transfer of college credits. The main problem with attending college under a new identity is getting credit for courses you've already taken. Obviously, you can't walk into the admissions department and say, "Oh, by the way, I've already earned an associate's degree under my previous identity." Unless you happen to work at a college and have the ability to do some mucking about in its computer systems, receiving credit for your previous education is not an option.

College-level proficiency examinations. These are tests offered by colleges where you can receive credit for knowledge you already have, regardless of how you obtained it. You may have to pay for the testing and the credits.

Credit by exam. If you convince your professor that you don't need to take his course because you already know the material, he may allow you to "test out" of the course. You will be given something similar to a final examination and, if you score high enough, you will be given credit for the course. Again, you may still have to pay for the credits.

Advanced placement. After you register with a college, you may be given a battery of placement tests. This is especially true of colleges that specialize in music, the arts, or engineering. This is often the best way to advance quickly because you will be given credit for any prerequisite classes you are allowed to skip due to successful placement testing. You usually do not have to pay for these credits.

Portfolio-based assessments. Off-campus colleges such as Regent's College will often grant credit based on your presentation of a portfolio. For example, to earn a humanities credit for an off-campus photography class, you will have to bring your photography portfolio to a professor and explain how you made the photographs and why they are artistically significant. The professor will then grade you based on his assessment of your presentation.

Telecourses. Some colleges, especially community colleges, will allow you to earn credit by watching certain PBS television series. To obtain the credit, you will eventually have to sit for a proctored examination on campus or at some facility designated by the college.

Correspondence courses. This is yet another distance-learning option where you receive study materials via mail, are given time to complete the projects, and then send them back to the school. This process continues, usually at the student's pace. To receive credit, you will have to eventually sit for a proctored exam as described above.

Independent study. This is where you're given a syllabus and allowed to study on your own using your own sources of study materials. Eventually, within a liberal time frame, you set up a proctored examination with the college.

Community college courses. I mention these because community colleges are often less strict in allowing credits to transfer between institutions, so you can jump from school to school if you happen to have a need to move about.

Online courses. Now that the World Wide Web is completely woven into the fabric of our society, more and more colleges are offering courses online. You meet online with the instructor and other classmates at a certain time and hold class via a chat room. Or sometimes the material is left available online in forum format, and the professor and classmates post in the forum at their convenience rather than in real time. The University of Phoenix was one of the pioneers of online study. Since I believe online study may interest many readers of this book, I've included a brief section below about the University of Phoenix's online degree program.

University of Phoenix

According to its Web site, the University of Phoenix was one of the first accredited universities to offer online degree programs to students, beginning this service in 1989. Today it offers bachelor's, master's, and doctoral degrees online, including: [1]

- Bachelor of Science in Business/Accounting
- Bachelor of Science in Business/Administration
- Bachelor of Science in Business/e-Business
- Bachelor of Science in Business/Management
- Bachelor of Science in Business/Marketing
- Bachelor of Science in Criminal Justice Administration
- Bachelor of Science in Health Care Services
- Bachelor of Science in Information Technology
- Bachelor of Science in Management
- RN to Bachelor of Science in Nursing
- Doctor of Business Administration
- Doctor of Education in Educational Leadership
- Doctor of Management in Organizational Leadership

With a computer, phone connection, and Internet Service Provider, you can work at your own rate, anywhere, anytime, to complete 100 percent of your education. The university provides easy-to-use software to help you retrieve lectures and assignments. You review the material off-line in text form so you don't have to worry whether your computer has the right version or the right word processor. You can access the university's online research library, interact with professionals, share ideas, debate issues, and learn from others' experience. There is an online instructor who checks your progress, providing feedback and guidance.

Classes are not held in "real time," so you'll never have to rush to get home or to a computer at a certain time. If your computer crashes or needs repair or your Internet connection goes down, you can pick up where you left off when your access problems are solved.

The university offers online courses one at a time, over a period of five or six weeks, for more in-depth study of each subject. You can take breaks between courses if you need to.

Visit their Web site at www.phoenix.edu for more information.

PART TWO: EMPLOYMENT

By establishing a business entity, the identity changer can appear to own, be associated with, or be employed by a business.

Establishing a business entity could be useful during job hunts when a potential employer is seeking a reference. Naturally, an identity changer does not want to use past jobs associated with his prior identity as references. This presents a problem. Although you may be qualified to do a certain job, there is nobody who will verify your past employment history. This is the same situation you were in when you first joined the workforce. The difference is that everybody expects a 17-year-old kid to be looking for experience and a first job. Most of you reading this book look much older than 17, and any potential employer is going to expect that you've already established some work history for yourself.

Here is a quick-and-dirty way to set up a business in order to use it as a job reference.

- Decide upon a business entity with which you would like to be associated.
- Establish a name, address, and phone number for that business.
- Go on your job interviews late in the day so you can be in the "office" with your voice changer (see Chapter 4) the next day when the potential employer calls to verify your previous experience.
- When the employer calls the next day to check your references, have your "secretary" verify your excellent work history.

Incidentally, some answering services will answer your line any way you like and regurgitate anything you tell them to. This is yet another alternative, but it is not nearly as impressive as the method outlined above. People can tell when they have reached an answering service!

Being associated with a business either as an owner or an employee has other advantages. For instance, maybe you don't even need a job. Maybe you're independently wealthy and desire to change your identity in order to better handle those nasty quarterly tax payments. Or perhaps you need to escape that ever-extending list of relatives who come sprawling and crawling, looking to sink their tiny, undeserving stubs into your hard-earned dough. In any case, if you've no need for a job, you may have considered skipping this chapter. Before you skip ahead, though, read on a bit. Even if you don't need gainful employment, learning how to create the illusion of having it will prove useful to you in your identity-changing endeavors. Remember, the goal of an alternate identity is to create the impression that you are a hardworking, upstanding citizen ready to participate in the social betterment of your community. Therefore, appearing to be employed, whether or not you actually are, can only serve you in this regard.

TYPES OF BUSINESS ENTITIES

Business entities can take the following forms:

- Sole Proprietorship
- Partnership
    (1) Limited Partnership
    (2) Family Limited Partnership
- Corporation
    (1) For Profit Corporation
    (2) Nonprofit Corporation
- Limited Liability Company
- Business Trust

• ⤸

Each of these entities has its own advantages and disadvantages. The advantages are inherent to the entity itself but also contain a subset of ramifications for the identity changer. Thus, we will not only explore the traditional advantages and disadvantages of the various forms, we will also discuss the special advantages and disadvantages as they pertain to identity changing.

Sole Proprietorships

A sole proprietorship is a business that is owned by an individual. He or she is personally liable for the income taxes and debts of the business. The individual may conduct business under his or her own name or under a fictitious name. If a sole proprietorship is to be conducted under a name other than the owner's real name, then the owner must file a "fictitious name statement" in the city or town where the business is located. This statement is typically referred to as a "DBA," which stands for "doing business as." A typical DBA statement would have the heading, "Theodore Thumbless D/B/A Fireworks R Us."

This statement puts the public on notice that the owner is conducting business under a name other than his real name. Also, all inquiries, comments, complaints, and service of process regarding said business may ultimately be directed to or served upon the owner of record.

The advantage of the sole proprietorship is its ease of start-up and lack of red tape. The disadvantage is that the person who starts the business must accept full liability for all claims brought against the business. Therefore, if the business is sued and it doesn't have enough assets to pay the court settlement, the plaintiff can look to the owner's personal assets and estate to collect the judgment.

Sole proprietorships have limited use to the identity changer. Typical uses would be mail anonymity and free magazine subscriptions. I suppose that a DBA could be used as supporting evidence for identity when opening bank accounts, although I've never found this necessary. In any case, the town clerk will ask you for identification when you fill out the DBA paperwork.

A sole proprietorship can open a bank account without a Social Security Number, which many readers may find handy. You will first need to apply to the IRS for an Employer Identification Number (EIN), also known as a Taxpayer Identification Number (TIN), or colloquially as an "04 number" because they used to all begin with 04, though this is no longer the case. Most sole proprietors use their SSN as their TIN, but if you hire employees, you must have an EIN. However, there is no reason you can't use an EIN even if you don't yet have employees.

The EIN is a business entity's equivalent of a SSN, and it is the number that banks and creditors will require of you when transacting business. Any form of business organization, including a sole proprietorship, may apply for an EIN.

To apply for an EIN from the IRS, a business entity uses Form SS-4. The IRS requires the person filling out the form to furnish their SSN for the IRS records. Do not worry too much about this part; it is only a precautionary measure taken by the IRS. Be sure to use the techniques from Chapter 3 to furnish them with a valid SSN just for good measure. As long as your business never gets into any trouble, the IRS will have no need to check out the SSN that you give them. It will not become a matter of public record, and creditors will never find it in any database.

Partnerships

A partnership, as its name implies, is a business entity established by two or more individuals known as partners. This arrangement is often referred to as a general partnership.

Unless otherwise agreed upon, partnerships formed by two individuals will give each individual a 50 percent share in the business as well as 50 percent of the voting power. Similarly, a partnership formed by three individuals will give each partner a one-third share and voting interest in the business. Most states recognize this default partnership status unless a contract between the partners specifically calls for a different arrangement.

The partnership is somewhat more of an entity unto itself than is the sole proprietorship. The partners must vote and decide on business matters, but each partner is still ultimately responsible for the taxes and debts of his share of the business. This means that creditors may look to the individual partners to satisfy debts if the partnership itself becomes insolvent. There must be a better way . . . .

Limited Partnerships

The limited partnership is a statutory entity allowing third parties, sometimes called "silent partners," to invest in a partnership with limited liability. Generally speaking, a limited partner is only liable to the partnership to the extent of his investment. In other words, if a limited partner invests $50,000 in a business and the business becomes insolvent, the limited partner can only lose $50,000. A limited partner cannot have his personal assets attached to satisfy claims against the partnership.

Limited partnerships are controlled by statute. In most states the statute is based, in whole or in part, on the Uniform Limited Partnership Act. There are certain requirements that must be met in order for the limited partnership to be valid. The main requirements are:

- An agreement, usually referred to as a Certificate of Limited Partnership, must be in writing and filed with the appropriate state agency (usually, the recorder's office in the county where the partnership is located, or the Secretary of State's office). This agreement in itself must also meet certain statutory requirements in order to be valid.
- Limited partners may not have control over the business.

- Limited partners may not include their name in the title of the partnership.

A good book on this subject (and asset protection in general) is *Lawsuit and Asset Protection* by Vijay Fadia, published by Homestead Publishing Company, Inc. Mr. Fadia's book was still in print when *The Modern Identity Changer* was first released. If you have trouble finding a copy, try looking for it through www.abebooks.com, www.bibliofind.com, or other online out-of-print book search services. You might get a better price if you find it on eBay.com or half.com.

A limited partnership offers certain advantages to the identity changer:

- Several paper identities can be set up as limited partners. In turn, these partners can hold assets for you in the event your main identity (general partner) gets into any legal trouble.
- The limited partnership can file for a TIN from the IRS (form SS4) and open one or more bank accounts. There is no need to give the bank any Social Security Number!
- The limited partnership can hire employees and give them W2 or 1099 forms at the end of the year. This places identities (and their Social Security Numbers) in the government's computers—a good way to "establish" an otherwise properly created new identity.

Although creditors cannot legally take a partner's interest to satisfy the partner's personal debts, a court may grant the creditor a "charging order" to attach the debtor partner's interest in the partnership. Unless unusually large sums of money are involved, creditors generally steer clear of trying to obtain charging orders because it is not economically feasible to do so.

Additionally, a savvy debtor can maintain full control of his assets by making himself the general partner of the partnership with an ownership interest of 5 percent and a controlling interest of 100 percent. If the partnership happens to make a profit in any given quarter, the general partner can elect to not distribute dividends. Even if a creditor takes the time and is lucky enough to get a charging order against the general partner's 5 percent interest in the partnership, he cannot collect on undistributed income. Moreover, the creditor now owns the general partner's tax position on the undistributed income. The general partner is obligated to send the creditor an IRS K-1 form declaring his undistributed gain and the creditor is obliged to pay tax on it! As you can see, it is not in the creditor's best interest to pursue charging orders against a debtor's share of a limited partnership.

So if your privacy concerns include an unhealthy portion of financial woes, you can use some of Big Brother's laws to keep him off your back until the statute of limitations runs out on whatever debt you owe (six years in most states).

Corporations

Once formed, a corporation is an entity unto itself. It is owned by shareholders and controlled by a board of directors. The corporation may file for a TIN, open bank accounts, conduct business, file lawsuits, and be sued in the name of the corporation. The formation, control, and operation of corporations are governed by statutes and regulations, which differ from state to state.

One disadvantage of the corporation is that the various states require a filing fee upon its establishment and also require annual reports to be filed, which also involve fees. Another disadvantage is the corporation's susceptibility to double taxation. The corporation, as an entity unto itself, is taxed, and then the shareholders, upon receiving dividends, are taxed again. However, certain small corporations can avoid this double taxation by filing as "S" corporations.

The advantages of a corporation, as distinguished from a limited partnership or business trust (described below), are:

- Legal in every state
- Esteem associated with the word "corporate"
- Business form is readily accepted by government and general public

The main advantage of a corporation, however, is that the shareholders are shielded from personal liability in suits brought against the corporation.

The big benefit to the identity changer is that the corporation can have a bank account in its own name with its own TIN. This is a better alternative to playing the Social Security game with the feds. It's much safer and, if done right, perfectly legal. However, unless you keep large sums of money on deposit, bank accounts for corporations usually carry higher monthly fees, and account activity is assessed a per-check and/or per-deposit surcharge. However, for the safety and peace of mind achieved, it is well worth it.

Nevada/Delaware Corporations

So what's all this hype about Nevada and Delaware corporations, anyway? Incorporating in these two states is thought to have certain advantages to those of us interested in privacy. This is true to an extent; however, many of the claims made by "incorporating services" in these states also hold true in many other states. Typical claims include:

- Shareholders are not a matter of public record
- One person may hold all officer and director positions
- No minimum corporate bank account
- No income tax
- Incorporators do not have to visit or reside in the state
- Ability to incorporate by phone or mail

All these conveniences are fine and dandy, but many other states offer some or all of these same advantages. Without going into a lot of detail about Nevada and Delaware corporations, I will tell you that their two best features are:

• One person may hold all officer and director positions
• No income tax

Although other states may have these advantages, many of the more densely populated states do not. Certainly, it is a great advantage to the identity changer if he or she can hold all officer and director positions. This eliminates the need to forge extra signatures or seek out associates.

The state of Nevada is virtually tax free. It does have a Nevada business tax, but organizations without employees are exempt from paying it. If, for some reason, you do wish to declare employees in Nevada, the tax is $25 per employee, per year; there are no other taxes that the corporation needs to worry about. A smart businessperson might use the Nevada corporation as a wholesaler, distributor, leasing agent, lending institution, advertising agent, management company, and home office for all invoices to avoid taxes and move income to a tax-free state.

Limited Liability Companies

Because they were new, controversial, and unsupported by statute, Limited Liability Companies (LLCs) did not make the cut for this book's original release. They have since come into wide acceptance, and I believe they are here to stay, mostly because lawyers and crooked politicians love them. Briefly, here's how they work.

You'll remember from above that a corporation protects its officers and shareholders from personal liability in the event the corporation is sued. The main downside is that the corporation is subject to double taxation. A partnership doesn't have the taxation problem, but the individual partners are left open to personal liability if their business is sued.

A properly formed LLC is like having the best of both worlds: liability of the business is limited to the business assets, leaving the business owners, who are essentially partners, protected from personal liability. The LLC itself is not taxed (as a corporation would be) but rather each partner pays his own taxes on any income earned through the entity.

Trusts

Often enigmatic, even to the people who use them, trusts can be understood if you take the time to examine their varied uses. Perhaps one reason why trusts are so mysterious is because there are several types, and most people don't understand their differences. In fact, most do not know that there are any differences.

The various forms of trusts are:

- Living
- Testamentary
- Revocable
- Irrevocable
- Land
- Realty
- Business

Don't skip ahead yet! I'm not going to burden you with detailed explanations of all these variations. Most of them are useless to the identity changer anyway. I merely list them here for the sake of completeness and for your own future reference.

Briefly, the first four trusts—living, testamentary, revocable, and irrevocable—are used primarily for estate planning, which is beyond the scope of this book. Land and realty trusts are essentially the same thing and may or may not have any distinction from any other trust, depending on what state you're in.

This leaves the business trust. The business trust may be very useful to the identity changer, indeed. First, some basics about trusts.

The basic form of any type of trust agreement is essentially the same. The main parts are:

- *Trustor*—The person who creates the trust by transferring property to the trustee.
- *Trustee*—The person who "cares for" the trust property.
- *Beneficiaries*—The people who have actual ownership interest in the trust property.

One person may be trustor, trustee, and beneficiary simultaneously. However, courts in most jurisdictions will dissolve such a trust to satisfy judgment creditors of the trustor.

The Business Trust

A business trust is a little-known form of business organization still perfectly legal in many states. Many years ago, investors in Massachusetts were not permitted to form corporations for the purpose of real estate acquisition and development. The Massachusetts Business Trust was born out of efforts by investors to circumvent statutes regulating corporations. The investors wanted to create a device whereby they could protect themselves from personal liability in the real estate business. Trusts were formed as an alternative, and their structure was upheld by courts and common law without the necessity of enacting statutes.

Trustee: A Trustee sits on the Board of Trustees and votes on matters before the Trust, much like a director in a corporation.

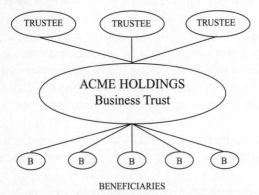

Business Trust: A stand-alone entity, just like a person, that can conduct business, hold title to property, maintain bank accounts, and assert or defend itself in civil court actions. Persons having claims or judgments against the Trust may only look to the Trust Property for payment.

Beneficiaries: A Beneficiary is a person who owns shares of the Trust and thus has a Beneficial Interest in the Trust Property. A Beneficiary has no control over the Trust other than to elect Trustees.

Courts have also upheld that the formation and use of business trusts was not limited to real estate investing. In this regard, the Massachusetts Business Trust became a common law device whereby a business could be formed, limiting liability to its shareholders (beneficiaries of the trust) and avoiding the taxes, fees, and regulation of the corporate structure.

As you may have already guessed, the IRS has enacted laws to make sure that these entities are taxed as corporations, and courts in several states have failed to recognize the Massachusetts Business Trust as a vehicle to limit investor liability. Some states, most notably Washington, fail to recognize business trusts altogether.

The good news is that there are still many states that continue to recognize the business trust, now often referred to as the "common law trust," as a completely valid business entity. Among these states are California, Illinois, Maryland, Massachusetts, Michigan, New Jersey, New York, Pennsylvania, West Virginia, and Wisconsin. A few states have even enacted statutes to protect this form of business organization. Massachusetts, of course, is one such state. California and Wisconsin are two others.

Arizona, Indiana, Kansas, Kentucky, Louisiana, and Texas have all adopted special rules for dealing with business trusts. If you're looking to set up in one of these states, you will want to review the laws and case histories of that particular state.

In Arkansas, California, Illinois, Massachusetts, Missouri, New York, and Rhode Island, beneficiaries who retain little or no control over the operation of a business trust are, in most circumstances, exempt from personal liability to the trust.

A business trust, like any other form of business entity, may apply for a TIN, open a bank account, and conduct business in the name of the trust. These trusts can be a great advantage to the identity changer because ownership of real, personal, and business property can be held anonymously in trust, with the identity changer, or third party, acting as trustee. If you exercise a certain amount of cunning as an identity changer, you can convince a bank, trust institution, or attorney to act as trustee for your trust. Your name will never appear anywhere in public record. Thus, creditors and investigators of your current or past identity will have no way of knowing that you have any assets to attach, nor will your name be gratuitously supplied to the various databases that we have discussed throughout this book.

Purchasing Property

When considering some of the tactics in Chapter 4, "Establishing Residence," you may wish to consider a common law trust as an investment vehicle, depending on your needs. They can often offer the ultimate in anonymity in states where it is legal to place real estate assets in a trust with undisclosed beneficiaries. In a trust with undisclosed beneficiaries, a statement called the Schedule of Beneficiaries is filed with the trustee. As its title implies, the schedule lists the beneficiaries of the trust. In some states, this paper does not need to be filed with the registrar of deeds. This is what you want.

There are also some states that distinguish a regular trust agreement from a real estate trust agreement. In these states, a trust where real estate is the only asset is known as a land trust. This type of trust is only permitted in a few states. If your state does not permit land trusts, then you will want to establish a standard business trust in which you will place personal property as well as real property.

At this point you're probably asking, "Who should be the trustee?" This is a good question. In most cases it will be your new identity, in one capacity or another, who signs the papers at the closing of the real estate transaction. This does not mean that your new identity has to act as trustee.

To take anonymity a step further, it would be nice to have a corporation act as trustee of your trust. Your new identity could now be acting as an officer of the corporation. The advantage of having a corporation act as trustee is that your identity will not be placed in an index at the registry of deeds.

Mixing all of the above ingredients, you can create the perfect hideout for yourself. Here is a step-by-step process that I have followed successfully. You will want to check the applicable laws of your target state before attempting this.

- Contact a Realtor and say you are interested in purchasing a bank-owned condo cheaply and quickly. Be sure to use your assumed identity.
- When you find a condominium that you like, make a cash offer that is 30 percent less than the bank's asking price and promise a fast closing. Banks like cash, and they will be anxious to get the white elephant off their books.
- The bank will counteroffer with a price $500 to $1,000 higher than your offer just to save face. Accept this offer.

At this point, the real estate agent will put you in touch with the bank's attorney. Tell her that the property will actually be deeded into a trust and that you will furnish her with a copy of the trust at the closing, although some attorneys won't even insist on this because some states do not require a trust agreement to be recorded with a real estate transaction. (In states where trusts are required to be recorded, it's best to have the trust set up and recorded with the county prior to the closing.)

The attorney will need the name of the trust as well as the name of the trustee (which could be a corporation) in order to prepare the title. Have this information ready. You may call the trust anything you like. Many people simply name the trust after the address of the property, such as 123 Easy Street Trust. The trustee is the person who must appear at the closing. If the trustee is a corporation, then an authorized officer of the corporation will have to appear.

Playing the Part

When you are purporting to be a business—whether a sole proprietorship, partnership, corporation, LLC, or trust—it is not only important that you meet all of the statutory filing requirements, you must also carry out the business as a business truly would. This means that you must file for your Tax Identification Number as soon as the business is established. You must pay business bills out of the business account and personal bills out of your personal account (or, at least, appear to do so). You must pay employees if the business claims to have them, file tax returns, and make payments toward loans or mortgages for which your business claims to be liable.

This is important because investigators for the IRS, bankruptcy trustees, and creditors look for this kind of consistent behavior when doing business with you or investigating you. Additionally, courts will look for this type of consistent business behavior when investigating creditor claims that the business is a sham or a fraud. In short, if you say you're a business, act like a business. This is the best protection you could ever have.

SELF-EMPLOYMENT: THE ROAD TO TRUE PERSONAL FREEDOM

Being self-employed and an entrepreneur at heart, it's difficult for me to not let my bias on this issue enter into this book. The question is, if you're not working for yourself, then who are you working for?

Think about how society is fed to us and the things that led you to read this book. Corporate America has an ingenious way of keeping the masses busy. An entry-level job in a corporation typically yields the young college grad somewhere between $20,000 to $30,000 per year. The corporate débutante is rather pleased with earning this salary. He'll casually slip it in at social gatherings, e.g., "Well, my wife and I discussed it and we had decided to hold out for twenty-five, but during my last interview the senior executive mentioned that the benefits were quite extensive, so I settled for twenty-four." The "thousand" is always implied in these conversations.

At the time of his first "real" job offer, the débutante resides in a modest apartment with his wife, and the new job can mean only one thing: it's time to buy a "home." Well, any good citizen knows that you simply can't go out, purchase a house, and live in it. First you must be prequalified, which is an interesting practice. Prequalification is a way for Corporate America to determine exactly how much money it can suck out of you without causing you to become insolvent. At the end of prequalification, the applicant is told he should be buying a home in the $130,000 to $140,000 price range. Ninety-nine percent of all junior corporate members blindly follow the home-buying process, from prequalification to closing. When it's all over, they wonder why they are struggling to keep up with payments, property maintenance, job requirements, and social life.

This struggling to keep up with everything is really just a way to keep you busy until you die. Corporations like to keep the masses concerned with things such as weight, appearance, health, social status, and, most of all, net worth. (I have heard people ask, "I wonder what my net worth is?" I would suggest that a person's "net worth" is very low if they think that it can be measured in terms of dollars.) In this way, Corporate America ensures that you will have no initiative of your own, whatsoever, outside of keeping up with Mr. Jones next door.

You see, corporations don't want people getting their own ideas and becoming the competition. Government does not want people getting together and becoming politically active. The status quo must be preserved so that those who are munching on a big piece of pie may continue munching on that pie. The masses must be led to believe that the leftover crumbs are magnanimous profferings from above and are more than enough to sustain them.

This is not to say the corporate route should be totally eliminated. If you are to gain true personal freedom, however, climbing the corporate ladder should be a means to an end. In essence, you should use the corporation as a path to your ultimate goal instead of letting the corporation use you.

· ◞

If you opt to not work for yourself but use the corporation to obtain your personal goals, you may be met with two
seemingly impenetrable barriers—education and experience.
Past work experience can be "obtained" by using the job front
methods outlined earlier. And there are a couple of ways
around the education problem.

If you are extremely knowledgeable in your profession and
can readily demonstrate this, many corporations may not care
if you hold an actual degree. Case in point: Bill Gates, co-
founder and largest shareholder of Microsoft Corporation. In
case you make your home immediately below a large moss-
bearing rock, I'll tell you that Microsoft Corporation has the
distinction of owning the rights to the operating system in
almost every IBM-compatible personal computer sold in
today's market.

It seems that some years ago, while Mr. Gates was
attending Harvard, he became aware of an opportunity in
the computer industry. He dropped out of college to pursue
this opportunity. Not long after that, IBM, anxious to get
into the personal computer craze, was pursuing Bill Gates.
Despite his apparent lack of college credentials, Gates
entered into a contract with IBM. At the time, some said
he'd signed on with the devil. But Gates gambled that
upstart companies would reverse-engineer IBM compatible
machines, which they eventually did in huge quantities. The
Gates-IBM contract did not restrict Gates' company,
Microsoft, from selling its operating system to these upstart
companies. IBM missed Bill's chess move, and it was check-
mate. Mr. Gates has since blown them out of the water, leaving them stuck with their bulky mainframes and forever
locked out of the personal computer market.

So if you have some special ability, don't be afraid to
approach a corporation with an offer of your own. To protect
your past identity, a little well-mannered attitude will go a
long way. If questions arise, simply remind them that you have
a special ability and you are wondering if your services will be
needed. Beyond that, you're not willing to indulge them.

If you don't have enough confidence in your abilities to pull off the above approach, a little educational background would certainly aid you in your job search.

Be Your Own Boss

Let's assume you're disgusted with Corporate America so much that you don't even want to use it as a means to an end. How do you make your own way in the world? Maybe you have an idea but will need a lot of start-up capital. What can you do for now, just to start earning some money?

Chapter 8 of my book *Identity, Privacy, and Personal Freedom: Big Brother vs. The New Resistance* offers 20+ pages of "tax free" ideas for the burgeoning entrepreneur or anyone who wants to make a buck, even while living under a new identity. I've listed just a few below. You could read that book, which contains more examples. It also has detailed descriptions of how you might bootstrap yourself up from ground zero by doing such things as recycling metals or collecting returnable cans and bottles. You could also research these and other ideas on your own.

- Actor
- Apartment broker
- Landscaper
- Investor
- Construction contractor
- Paper deliverer
- Private detective
- Street vendor
- Writer

SUMMARY

This chapter is filled with a lot of legal and technical information with which any identity changer should become familiar. By having a better understanding of the legal, social,

• ⤳

and economic foundations of the business community, the identity changer will gain an advantage when working and residing within that community.

If most of this information is new to you, I recommend you reread this chapter at a later date. When you are finally comfortable with all of the above topics, you can then research your state statutes and case histories at your local library or through the Internet. By doing this, you will become more knowledgeable than most businesspersons in your community. Armed with that knowledge, you will become more powerful and enjoy an advantageous position. Knowledge is power. Now, you can create or find meaningful employment for your new identity.

ENDNOTE

1. Source: University of Phoenix Web site, www.phoenix.edu.

CHAPTER SIX

Homemade Identity Documents

᠆᠂

In this book's original 1997 edition, I'd included a chapter entitled "Making a Work ID." It was a simple chapter illustrating how you could use everyday household tools and materials to construct an employee's ID card. A private detective could use such an ID to support a ruse, or a privacy seeker might use one to open a bank account under an assumed name.

There are many laws pertaining to the construction of ID cards, and the ID card artisans among us must be careful to not throw themselves headlong into Big Brother's legalistic web. There are certain things ID makers can legally do and certain things that can land said artisans in the Inner Party prison system for many years. As of this writing, I'm pretty sure it's okay to think about making ID cards, and I'll go out on a limb and say that it's okay for me to write about it. But please be advised that all laws are subject to change at a moment's notice at the whim of bureaucrats who believe in serializing human beings at birth. Our discussion will therefore center around *novelty IDs,* which for the moment at least appear to be tolerated, if not actually sanctioned, by the establishment.

Even though six years have passed since this book's first printing, I still think that the original "Making a Work ID" chapter has merit. It illustrates many of the old-school techniques used in novelty ID manufacture, and I've always believed that spending some time in the School of Hard

Knocks is the best way to develop appreciation for the short-cuts and quantum leaps in quality that modern technology has allowed. So if you have a copy of this book's original edition, please don't completely discount the "Making a Work ID" chapter. But because this is a revised and expanded edition, I have decided to completely update this chapter and show you some tricks from another book I've since written titled *Secrets of a Back-Alley ID Man: Fake ID Construction Techniques of the Underground.*

THE DRIVER'S LICENSE

If you've read books like this one before, you've heard it a million times: The driver's license has become the de facto national ID card. Chapter 3, "Identity Documents," shows you how to go about getting an actual state-issued driver's license.

But maybe you don't want to invest that much time. Maybe you just need a novelty driver's license to cash your paycheck or get a big-city library card. My book *Secrets of a Back-Alley ID Man* contains detailed instructions for con-structing various state driver's licenses, complete with security signatures, seals, holograms, and laminates. I have chosen to reprint a section of it here, which contains a little taste of everything in that book: a bit of new technology, old-school construction methods, and good ol' poor man's techniques. Holograms, lamination, and modern equipment to help con-struct novelty IDs are also discussed in detail in that text.

Remember the Maine! Er, I Mean, Why Maine?

The current Maine driver's license is the age-old basic lam-inated card with repetitive lettering. It is one of only a handful remaining that can be produced entirely by old-school meth-ods. I will use it to demonstrate a few such techniques.

Maine template. You do not have to worry too much about the corners or edges at this point. These will be trimmed in the final step.

Place template in typewriter and type away. Keep in mind that Maine has a seven-digit license number and a six-year term expiring on the applicant's birthday. Issue date may be before birthday.

MAINE DRIVERS LICENSE

ISSUED	EXPIRES	CLASS
1/1/01	1/1/07	C

LICENSE NO	BIRTHDATE
1234567	1/1/41

RESTRICTIONS	ENDORSEMENTS
BCMS	My Mom

HAIR	EYES	HEIGHT	WEIGHT	SEX
SOME	WH	8'12"	111	Y

SIGNATURE

CHARRETT, SHELDON
704 HOUSER ST.
BRONX, ME 10011

Secretary of State
Dan Gwadosky

Place passport photo or other self-portrait in appropriate corner, overlay the seal/signature/camera number transparency, press it all together with a pane of glass, and take exposures from varying distances to ensure that you get a proper-sized print back from the developer.

"Hand-Drawn" Template

The Maine template is very basic. It can be drawn by hand or possibly made with transfer lettering. For our purposes, and because I am not a good drawer, I made a computer-generated template. But you can see where artistically inclined people could readily draw this with pen and ink. Those with good Dumpster-diving skills could dig a blank information card from behind a Maine DMV. You can make the seal, signature, and camera number overlay in a word processor file, then print it directly onto a transparency. If your printer doesn't like transparencies, you could print it to paper and then photocopy the page onto a transparency (copy shops will do this for you).

Refer to the above photo and caption. The entire assembly was "shot down" using a 200mm micro lens. To get the end product the correct size, I had to shoot it fully zoomed out

Do-it-yourself stamping kit. Arrange the letters to say "STATE OF MAINE." Use narrow spacers to minimize the length. The font is very close to the actual font used. Most bureaucrats won't notice the difference.

A mock-up printing press to transfer the repetitive pattern onto the lamination pouch or transparent insert. Rub only the slightest amount of Interference Gold onto the rubber stamp. If you make a mistake on one line, it's easy to erase it and redo.

from about 20 inches away. Different macros with different settings and focal ratios will produce different results. You must experiment on your own.

Security Pattern

The Maine driver's license has a repetitive security pattern on the lamination pouch. Fortunately, this security feature is a simple "STATE OF MAINE" pattern repeated in a straight column down the face of the laminated card. It is a standard Interference Gold color and effect. Again, a gifted artist could spend a few hours painting this in, but here are a few alternatives for the semi-gifted, the not-so-gifted, and the just plain brain-dead.

•⟶

Rubber Stamp

For about $20 you can have a rubber stamp made up that says STATE OF MAINE in a repeated column. Order it from another state and the person you speak with will probably have no idea why you want it but will be happy to take your $20. Alternatively, you could buy a do-it-yourself stamp kit for around $10. I have such a kit, and the font just so happens to be the right type, although a bit bigger. I doubt most bureaucrats would notice a larger font.

Gently brush Interference Gold acrylic paint onto either type of stamp with a foam applicator. Use a miniscule, almost invisible amount. At this point you have several options:

- Stamp a piece of Dura-Lar film, which you'll later lay over the printed ID template before laminating.
- Stamp an ID already laminated with a 5-mil pouch and then relaminate with another 5-mil pouch.
- Stamp a heat-laminated ID and then "cold-laminate" it with Super Clear cellophane tape.
- Stamp a laminated ID and then heat-laminate just the front using half a 5-mil pouch.

Remember that the repetitive STATE OF MAINE pattern extends to the very edge of the ID (not just to the edge of the visible template). Sometimes you must tear the fused edge of a lamination pouch to achieve this effect.

Some disadvantages of the do-it-yourself kit are as follows:

- You have to assemble the letters STATE OF MAINE yourself.
- You have to stamp the lamination pouch several times.
- You have to keep reapplying the Interference Gold paint to the stamp.
- You have to be very careful to keep the repetitive pattern in line.
- Once done, the letters are still slightly too big.

Repetitive lettering printed onto Dura-Lar and laid over a composite Maine ID card. Add a back, cut, and laminate for finished product.

Another Repetitive Lettering Method

You can print the repetitive pattern onto Dura-Lar (or an even thinner transparent film) using a Metallic Gold cartridge in an Alps printer. Here's the procedure:

1. Open Word or another word processing program and make 20 or more STATE OF MAINE lines.
2. Select all text and change to Arial 10-point font.
3. Change line spacing to .7. In Word choose Paragraph, Line Spacing, Multiple, and enter .7 into the box.
4. Select Print, Properties to get into the printer control window.

5. Now, you have to cheat a little by telling the printer you are using laser printer paper. Then select Spot Colors, Single Ink, Metallic Gold, and hit OK.
6. Load a transparency, Dura-Lar, or other transparent film into the printer and print.

You now have a repetitive pattern in gold ink that is way too dark to be believable.

Get the cleanest, finest piece of steel wool you can find and begin to gently efface the repetitive pattern. If you see immediate progress, you're pressing way too hard. Ease off and take your time. Work evenly on all parts of the repetitive pattern using a wide circular motion. After a while you'll begin to see the effect you're looking for. This is a crucial point because some areas will be more effaced than others. Once a letter is half erased, it does not take much to make it disappear completely. So now you have to be more selective with the steel wool. Gently rub only the areas that still need rubbing. Do not worry about the light scratches on the plastic (transparency, Dura-Lar, whatever). Those will be filled in by the vinyl chloride in the lamination pouch and will actually help keep air bubbles from forming.

You'll want to beat up the license a little when you're done. A supposedly four-year-old license is less believable if it is shiny and scratch free.

Another One

If the above repetitive lettering method sounds like more work than you want to get into, there is a much faster way. You can print directly to Dura-Lar or a transparency using a gold ink cartridge in an appropriate printer as described above, with one minor adjustment. First select all the text and choose Format, Font. Next to Color, choose 25 percent gray. Now print.

The downside to this method is that the gold ink does not offer a continuous tone. Rather, it prints the repetitive pattern

FONT INFO FOR MAINE

Section	Font
FIELDS	Arial Black, 5-point, bold Stretched vertically 1 to 2 pixels Compressed horizontal to actual width
DATA	Courier New, 8-point, bold Height stretched one or two pixels
SECRETARY OF STATE	Old English Text MT, 10-point, bold Stretched vertically 1 to 2 pixels Compressed horizontally to same length as original
"DAN GWADOSKY" (May differ depending on year)	Old English Text MT, 7-point, bold Stretched vertically 1 to 2 pixels Compressed horizontally to fit
CAMERA NUMBER	Courier New, 8-point, bold Stretched vertically 2 pixels

as a sparse series of dots. Upon close inspection, the dot pattern may look unnatural to a savvy clerk. This aside, I'd bet an otherwise well-made license using this repetitive lettering technique would work nine times out of ten in states other than Maine.

Choosing Outline under the Format Font menu results in a slightly different look (outline lettering), which also may work well in distant states.

And Another One

If you want to experiment with various shades of gold, there is yet another variation on this theme. You'll recall that Word gives you little choice as to the tone of gold; you can choose between 25 and 50 percent. The latter is way too dark for our purposes, so you really have no choice at all. While 25 percent seems to be just about right for Maine, you may desire to experiment with different gray-scale percentages when using this repetitive lettering technique, especially on other IDs.

Print out the repetitive pattern in black ink onto white laser printer paper and then scan the image back into your computer. This step ensures proper font size and letter spacing. If you were to capture the repetitive pattern directly from the screen, it would more than likely contain imperfections because even "true type" screen fonts are not so "true" once you play with character and line spacing. Now, import the scanned image into Word as a picture object and place the object in the header. Right-click the picture to edit its properties. Convert it to a "watermark" and then adjust the brightness and contrast to suit your needs. You can see where this gives you infinite control over the image's transparency.

If you have Photoshop, you can also import the image into its own layer of a .PSD file. Once done, it is a simple matter to experiment with different opacities to adjust the transparency of the pattern.

None of these repetitive lettering methods is perfect. But if you remember to beat up your ID real good when it's done, it will be believable. Steel wool is a good tool for aging an ID. You can use the foregoing methods for any ID that has repetitive gold lettering.

Computer Template Method

The Maine license is a good candidate for old-school construction methods, but you can also make one using the computer template method. Here is the font information for doing just that.

Stretching and Compressing Text

Making a Maine driver's license template offers a glimpse at yet another of Photoshop's powerful image manipulation routines. In the table on page 125, you'll note several instances where the text must be stretched or compressed. The actual term for this process is called "scaling." Other manipulation methods (described in *Secrets of a Back-Alley ID Man*) can be used, but sometimes scaling the text is faster, more efficient, and better looking.

Using the Maine Template

You can print out the final template as a large card for a composite photo ID or use Photoshop to fill in the data fields and print it out as a small card ready for backing and lamination.

ID Back

If you've ever scoured the Internet for high-quality driver's license templates, you know how frustrating it can be to find them. Many people end up paying for them and are still disappointed. It's even more frustrating when a good template does not include the back side! I find this exceedingly odd since one of the first things any decent ID checker does is turn the card over; in fact, sometimes this is the only thing a bureaucrat or clerk does to verify an ID. I often wonder what people do when they get Internet templates without backs. I sometimes envision their finished product with a Mickey Mouse or Donald Duck sticker on the back. I've included below and on the following pages some backs I've made or reworked on my computer.

RESTRICTION CODE	ENDORSEMENT CODE
A - CORRECTIVE LENSES	H - HAZARDOUS MATERIALS
B - DAYLIGHT OPERATION	I - MOTORCYCLE
C - DRIVER IMPROVEMENT	J - MOTOR DRIVEN VEHICLE
D - MOTORCYCLE	K - VALID UNTIL 30 DAYS AFTER DISCHARGE
E - MOTOR DRIVEN CYCLE	FROM ARMED FORCES
G - GEOGRAPHICAL	N - TANK VEHICLE
M - MEDICATION	P - PASSENGER (BUS) VEHICLE
R - MOPED	T - DOUBLE/TRIPLE TRAILER
Q - CONDITIONAL LICENSE	X - COMB. TANK HAZARDOUS MATERIALS
S - SPECIAL EQUIPMENT	Y - SCHOOL BUS OVER 15 PASSENGERS
W - OPERATION OF VEHICLES	Z - SCHOOL BUS 15 PASSENGERS OR
EQUIPPED WITH AIR	LESS INCLUDING DRIVER
BRAKES NOT ALLOWED	

PLACE ORGAN DONOR DECAL HERE

The actual text on the Maine license back is blue.

• ⌐

CLASS 1 ALL VEHICLES NOT EXCEEDING 24,000 LBS. GVW. EXCEPT MOTORCYCLES
CLASS 2 INCLUDES CLASS 1 AND SINGLE VEHICLES EXCEEDING 24,000 LBS. GVW. EXCEPT
MOTORCYCLES
CLASS 3 INCLUDES CLASS 1, 2 AND ALL VEHICLE COMB. EXCEEDING 24,000 LBS. GVW
EXCEPT MOTORCYCLES
CLASS 4 MOTORCYCLES
CLASS 5 MOPED

A	CORRECTIVE LENSES	E	NEIGHBORHOOD ONLY	J	AUTOMATIC TRANS.
B	SPECIAL RESTRICTED*		(10 MI. HOME)	K	POWER STEERING/BRAKES
C	NO INTERSTATE DRIVING	F	PREVIOUS DUI	L	OTHER
D	NOT TO EXCEED 50 MPH	G	HAND CONTROLS	M	OUTSIDE MIRROR
		H	STEERING KNOB	N	TURN SIGNALS

B*   SPEC. REST. (Age 15) MAY OPERATE 6 a.m. to 6 p.m. EXCEPT FOR DAYLIGHT SAVINGS
TIME 6 a.m. to 8 p.m. thur 8-31. 6 p.m. TO 6 a.m. ACCOMPANIED BY LICENSED DRIVER
OVER 21 OR LICENSEE'S PARENT OR GUARDIAN. FARM MACH. OR EQUIP (OTHER
THAN PASS. VEH.) MOTORCYCLES OF 6 BHP OR LESS AT AGE 16 BECOMES REG.
LIC. AND DOES NOT HAVE TO BE EXCHANGED UNTIL EXPIRATION.

(A)

This card is the official verification of your Social Security number. Please sign it right away. Keep it in a safe place.

Improper use of this card or number by anyone is punishable by fine, imprisonment or both.

This card belongs to the Social Security Administration and you must return it if we ask for it.

If you find a card that isn't yours, please return it to:
Social Security Administration
P.O. Box 17087, Baltimore, MD 21235

For any other Social Security business/information, contact your local Social Security office. If you write to the above address for any business other than returning a found card, it will take longer for us to answer your letter.

Social Security Administration
Form SSA-3000 (4-90)   D12345678

(B)

Various ID backs: (A) 1990 South Carolina driver's license; (B) a Social Security card, which crooks often find handy; (C) 1999 Illinois driver's license; and (D) a generic card back you can modify to your heart's content. If you download a backless template from the Internet (an annoying reality, I'm afraid), try using one of these backs in its place. Modify them as you see fit.

A license back can be scanned into Photoshop and reworked or used as-is if it's a good scan. But some of the cleanest license backs are laid out with and printed directly from a good word processor. A word processor file takes up far less memory than a high-resolution Photoshop or JPEG image. The Maine back shown on page 127 was mocked up in Word 97.

(C)

(D)

BUYING FAKE DRIVER'S LICENSES

Identity researchers have recently learned that the Internet is one of the best places to buy such fake ID as state driver's licenses. Unfortunately these Internet sites are short-lived. The proprietor of www.youneedone.com recently met with a considerable amount of Inner Party unpleasantness. For about

$50, the man, whom I shall call Crett Barreras, would make you a top-quality driver's license from any state, perfectly replicating even the most intricate credit card-style driver's licenses with complex repetitive rainbow holograms. Unfortunately, Crett was slammed with a crushing lawsuit and has had his site forced out of operation.

So what's an identity changer to do? Play "Beat the Feds," that's what. Find the Web sites of other "Cretts" before the government does. Use search engines, join newsgroups, ask questions. You'll find what you're looking for before too long.

What about those who are not computer-savvy? Er, the old standbys I suppose will do. I won't list them all, but you know . . . Blue Hill Avenue, Sunset Strip, Alvarado Street, Bonanza Road. You know which cities. If you don't, drive some night to the biggest city in your state and walk around till you hear someone scream, "Oh, my god, I'm being stabbed to death!" Walk toward the screaming—the gunshots should get louder; the body count should increase. Walk right to the center of the mayhem: that's where you begin your search.

PAPER DOCUMENTS

In a totalitarian society, one must have his papers in order. In this brave new world of credit card-style drivers' licenses and smart cards, it will soon be more appropriate to say that one must have his *plastic* in order. But there are still plenty of documents Big Brother has kept relegated to paper, at least for the time being. And of course, he has a way to protect the security of such paper documents. This section contains methods to appease Big Brother's desire for secure paper documents.

Raised Seal

My book *Secrets of a Back-Alley ID Man: Fake ID Construction Techniques of the Underground* contains methods for getting a raised seal on any paper document, including birth certificates and real estate deeds. To give you a basic idea of the techniques presented in that text, we have reprinted a short section of it here. *Back-Alley ID* goes on to discuss a cleaner method of lifting any kind of raised seal.

I Love Super Sculpey Method

Crafty grafters know about a nifty little product called Super Sculpey, available at any decent arts and crafts store. Sculpey is special sculpting putty that I've adapted to a special use. You can press Sculpey onto a three-dimensional object to make a perfect mold of it. Alternatively, you can press Sculpey into a mold to replicate a three-dimensional object.

A notary's embossing plate is a three-dimensional object, right? So, if you are lucky enough to be alone with a notary's

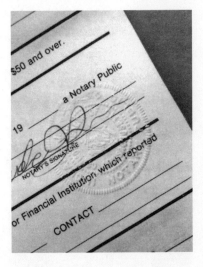

Notary embossed document seen from behind for clarity. Notice how this is a good, full impression. Some notaries have weak hands and give you lame impressions that aren't good enough for duplicating with the Super Sculpey method.

This is the same document as seen from the front. A silicone mold must be made from the front of a document.

Apply 100 percent silicone to front of document.

Use a disposable cup to press silicone into the notary impression. Do this gently and don't oversquish. Let it set for at least 24 hours.

Peel the paper from the dried silicone. Rub off the paper residue in warm soapy water. You now have a very durable mold of a notary seal.

Silicone molds of Connecticut, Massachusetts, and New York notary seals.

Press a warm ball of Sculpey into the mold. Do this as evenly as possible. You'll have to press harder than when you squished the silicone onto the paper, but you still don't want to flatten it completely.

Peel the mold from the Sculpey. Place the ceramic cup with Sculpey into the oven (see procedure above).

embosser for a few minutes, you could use Sculpey to make a mold of it.

Well gee, thanks, Charrett. When the hell will I ever be alone with a notary's embosser? You suck.

Now wait a minute there, cowboy, those is harsh words. The good news is that we ordinary schmucks—the ones who'll never have a snowball's chance in hell of ever being alone with a notary's embosser—can use Sculpey in a different way.

Although you wouldn't normally think of it as such, the impression an embosser makes onto a piece of paper is actually a mold, isn't it? Certainly even you have a notarized document somewhere in your house. No? Well then, it's a simple matter to go the city clerk's office and get something notarized. Make sure the notary squeezes that embosser tight so you have a nice mold to work from. Tell him or her that you need a strong impression so it shows up on the photocopy.

When you get home, take a 3/4-inch ball of Super Sculpey and work it in your hands until it is very warm, soft, and pliable. Then press it into the back of the embossed seal. Gently pull the paper from the Sculpey to reveal your new notary embossing plate. Bake it in the oven at 270 degrees for 15 minutes, or at a much lower setting (150–170 degrees) for a longer time. Serves one. Recipe may be doubled if you are expecting guests.

Once you pull Sculpey from the oven, let it cool for a couple hours. After that, your embossing plate should be hard and ready for service.

SUMMARY

The hard-core identity changer is going to seek solid, government-issued documents. There are various routes to obtaining these documents, depending on one's circumstances and needs, but the identity changer can use novelty IDs as a means to this end. This chapter showed you a few novelty ID construction methods and has provided you with resources for further study.

Privacy seekers may not necessarily need novelty IDs as a means to procure more official documents, but they might wish to possess certain documents to protect themselves from certain dangers in this hostile world, many of which I've listed in the book's introduction.

Chapter Seven

Banking

Considering all that we have covered in Chapters 3 and 5 on establishing Social Security Numbers, Employer Identification Numbers, and business entities, you may think that there is little left to be said on the subject of money. Granted, we have covered many legal aspects of handling finances, but there is more to consider beyond legalities. What of practicality? The following are some fine points that I, as a detective who has helped others disappear, have learned over the years.

PERSONAL ACCOUNTS

If all you need is a private bank account, the solution may be something as simple as using somebody else's. Once, I took over my father's bank account, complete with $1,000 in overdraft protection. He was retiring and moving to a more agreeable climate. He said, "Here you go."

At the time I was very young and had no credit, so this helped a great deal. I simply signed his name on the checks and no one was ever the wiser. Upon my father's death, I had the option of continuing to use the account (as well as several others) or closing them out so that my dad could rest in peace. I opted for the latter.

The point is, if you aren't planning on starting a new life but simply are in need of some financial privacy, there may be no need to get carried away with secret accounts, business entities, and SSNs. You just need to ask a close friend or trusted family member to open a checking account for your use.

You may wish to have your trusted friend or family member open a savings account for you instead and pay your bills by money order. Friends and family members may be more amenable to this idea because it eliminates the worry about you bouncing checks in their name and ruining their credit. Even people who trust you may prefer to be cautious.

Just be aware that Big Brother's widening eyes are now supported by big legislation. New banking laws require tellers to file a "Suspicious Activity Report" (SAR) with the feds if they spot what they consider to be unusual financial behavior from a customer. One money order per month from different banks and post offices would probably not raise any eyebrows . . . yet.

Unless you have good reason to do so and know precisely what you are doing, opening a personal bank account under an assumed identity may not be your securest option. Too many SSN databases exist, and too many laws are broken in the process. Moreover, security checks are being implemented and databases are growing at an exponential rate. What's safe today may not be safe tomorrow. For these reasons, opening a business account is preferable in most circumstances.

BUSINESS ACCOUNTS

When opening a business account, the bank representative will request some or all of the following documents:

Document	Source
Corporate Resolution	Corporate Directors Meeting
EIN (also called TIN) number	IRS Form SS-4
DBA Certificate	City/Town Hall
Business Address	Mail Drop/Residence
Business Telephone	Voice Mail/Answering Service
Declaration of Trust	You recorded this at the deeds registry

The exact requirements obviously will vary depending on the type of business entity opening the account. As a general rule, the documents you drew up to make your business "official" will probably be needed to open a business bank account.

Some banks are more lax than others on these requirements. In general, smaller banks in more rural areas are less restrictive in their requirements. Also, an extremely large initial deposit will cause a lot of bank representatives to turn their head to certain omissions. This is particularly true if the representative is heavily invested in the bank or working on commission.

Using a Check as ID

A wonderfully subtle form of ID when opening a business or any type of bank account is to have a check for the initial deposit that is made out to the person or business entity opening the account. The account representative will subconsciously assume that you're legitimate. After all, why would you have a check made out to you if you weren't you?

It's even better if the check is made out to you and your business. For example, a check payable to the order of "ACME BIRDSEED & GUNPOWDER, LTD., c/o Rowe D. Runner, CEO" looks very convincing.

The check should be drafted from a well-known business in the community. A favorite trick of mine is to go shopping for commercial office space, sign a lease, and put a deposit on a property that you like. Use the same alias or business name with which you will be opening your bank account. Most state laws allow a "no fault" termination of a lease whereby the leasee can terminate the lease, usually within three days, and request his or her deposit back. This renders the lease null and void, and there is nothing the rental agent can do about it. It's the law.

Because the rental agent is a big business, the money would have already been deposited into their bank account, and they are now required by law to issue you a check in the amount of your initial deposit.

• ⟶

Nothing looks better when you walk into a bank than to have a big check from a large, well-known, local business written out to you or your business entity (or both)! Be aware, however, that this might raise eyebrows in a small community, where people talk. Remember to adapt to your environment. In this case, the local business should be large enough to protect your anonymity, and the check amount should be in keeping with the income and spending habits of the area.

Advantages in Timing

Incorporating other tenets of human psychology can further reduce the difficulty you might encounter when attempting to establish a business or personal bank account.

If you walk into a bank when it is very busy, during lunchtime, or just prior to lunch or closing time, you will most likely be dealing with individuals who have temporarily relaxed their standards. Their mind is on getting caught up, eating lunch, going home, or whatever the case may be. During these times, they have a tendency to push things through in order to get on with their own lives that much quicker. Opening an account during periods when the bank is advertising for new accounts and/or offering incentives to their employees or customers for establishing new accounts is yet another advantage in timing available to the identity changer or privacy seeker.

Advantages in Psychology

Bank reps open dozens of personal accounts a week. When you go in to open a business account, the bank representative is often so preoccupied trying to remember that particular procedure that she pays much less attention to your personal credentials. The rep assumes your personal credentials are in order if you are opening up a business account.

Also, younger clerks make more mistakes. Keep that in mind during your travels.

Endorsing Business Checks

Another nice advantage of having a business account is that you will not have to throw your signature around. When you make deposits, you only need stamp the check:

For Deposit Only
ACME Birdseed, INC
ACCT# 012-34-5678

When writing checks to pay bills, you can use a rubber stamp signature. These can be made up for you at most print shops for about $15. Give the print shop a sample of "your" signature. If you are right-handed, make up a signature with your left hand. If you are left-handed, give them your best right-handed signature. Within an hour, you will receive a stamp that you can use over and over again.

To endorse checks for deposit, you can buy a rubber stamp kit and arrange the letters to say anything you want. This is good if you have several accounts. These kits also come in handy for other purposes, as you saw in Chapter 6 and will see in Chapter 9.

OPENING A BANK ACCOUNT WITHOUT AN SSN

You can legally open a bank account without a Social Security Number. Whether you can practically do so is another matter entirely. Like so many other facets of privacy and new ID, a lot depends on your ultimate goal. If you're trying to keep a low profile and live entirely under a new ID, it's probably best not to fight with bank bureaucrats, which you would have to do to keep your SSN out of their records. Why? Because despite the lack of legal necessity, banking institutions insist on your SSN anyway.

I cover this topic in detail in Chapter 10 of *Identity, Privacy, and Personal Freedom: Big Brother vs. The New Resistance*. It's too much information to reprint here, but I will highlight some key points.

There is no federal law or regulation requiring banks to have a customer's SSN. The relevant statutes only require banks to *make an effort to secure* customer SSNs for certain interest-bearing accounts. If the bank is unable to secure a customer's SSN or TIN, it is required to report this fact to the IRS along with the customer's name and address. That's the extent of the law. In fact, parts of the federal law specifically exclude a bank's necessity to even make the effort to determine a customer's SSN or TIN for certain types of accounts. Basically, any installment savings account expected to earn less than $10 interest per year is excluded from the above requirement. Also, banks need not make an effort to secure the SSN of certain temporary and nonresident aliens. It may be beneficial to renounce your U.S. citizenship, become a resident of another country (see Chapter 5 of *Identity, Privacy, and Personal Freedom: Big Brother vs. The New Resistance,* especially if you have Irish ancestry), and open a U.S. bank account as a nonresident alien.

If it's just privacy you're after and you don't mind fighting with bank bureaucrats, open a non-interest-bearing savings account and refuse to give them your SSN. They will fight you and probably refuse to open an account for you, but just keep coming back at 'em with the law. Tom Scambos, host of www.tax-freedom.com, has a whole bunch of forms and legal retorts to help citizens open up bank accounts without providing their SSN. Mr. Scambos has helped many people, and his Web site contains pages and pages of information invaluable to freedom-loving people. I highly recommend visiting www.tax-freedom.com and familiarizing yourself with rights you probably didn't even know you had.

ONLINE BANKING AND PAYMENT SERVICES

Online banks have exploded in popularity since this book's original release. As of this writing, you can still open an online bank account with no monthly fee and a $50 sign-up bonus. One such bank is www.netbank.com.

Aside from the incentives, online banks have all the requirements of their walk-in counterparts, so I won't say too much about them other than this: One can apply for accounts from the safety of a library or university computer. So if you happen to be living under an assumed or new identity, you don't have to worry about those embarrassing moments when the bank bureaucrat throws you a tough question that you can't quite handle. When applying online, it's a computer that rejects you. You can learn from your mistake and sit in front of the same computer and try again. Not true in the instance of making a bank rep suspicious.

Payment services such as PayPal, currently owned by eBay, have slightly more flexible sign-up requirements. They're not bank accounts exactly, nor do you need a bank account to sign up. If you happen to have credit under a new or assumed identity, you can use online payment services with your credit card.

Though PayPal is getting stricter, at one time I—or, er, rather a friend of mine—had several accounts under different aliases. At that time it did not matter whether the associated bank account or credit card information matched the PayPal account information. Keep an eye out for start-up online payment services that may at first be more lax in their standards.

PUTTING IT ALL TOGETHER

Using the above ideas and methods in concert will give you a comfortable advantage when dealing with bank bureaucrats. You will probably not need to use all of the above tricks to establish a bank account, but it is nice to have this information at your disposal. Armed with these advantages, you can select the concepts that apply to your particular situation and arrange your visit to the bank to allow the greatest chance of success. You want to be talking to the right clerk at the right time about the right things while possessing all of the necessary documentation that may be requested. Certainly, anybody who has done their homework to this extent will not be held in question.

If any questions or suspicions do arise, simply take your documents and your business elsewhere. You have not broken the law, and the clerk has no authority or jurisdiction over you other than to refuse to open an account. This is not a problem. There are hundreds of other banks to choose from.

CHAPTER EIGHT

Establishing Credit

Surely you have had occasion in your life to fill out a bank loan or credit card application. You probably even had a general idea of how the companies issuing the application would like you to respond. You may have even written down some little white lies in the hopes of being considered a better candidate for credit. Most folks can pretty much guess, for example, that the lending institution is more likely to issue credit to a person possessing a respectable annual salary. You've probably fudged the numbers once or twice, thinking, "Should I be doing this? Will they call my boss in the morning? Well, maybe I'll just exaggerate a little bit and hedge my bets. Why do they ask me if I have a telephone? Is that good or bad? What difference does it make if I'm married and have children? Job title? That shouldn't matter . . ."

The fact is, it all matters.

CREDIT PROFILES: WHAT CREDITORS LOOK FOR

Most creditors issue credit on a point scoring system. Every question on the application will be assigned a certain number of points depending on how it is answered. Below I've outlined a typical point system. Most companies will ask you questions hoping to obtain most or all of the following information:

• ↘

CATEGORY	POINTS ALLOTTED

Age Group of Applicant:

Under 25 years of age	1
26 to 45 years of age	3
46 to 64 years of age	2
65 or older	1

Residence:

Less than 1 year at current residence	0
1 to 5 years	1
5 to 10 years	2
Over 10 years	3

Less than 1 year at previous residence	0
1 to 5 years	1
Over 5 years	2

Profession:

Professional (doctor, lawyer, executive)	5
White Collar (sales, marketing, etc.)	4
Blue Collar (construction, plumbing, etc.)	3
Other	2
Self-employed	1

Time at Current Job:

Over 10 years	5
6 to 10 years	4
3 to 5 years	3
1 to 2 years	2
Less than a full year	1

Family Status:

Married	1–2
Spouse employed	1–2
1 or 2 dependent children	1–2

CATEGORY	POINTS ALLOTTED (con't)
No children	0
More than three children	0–1

Financial History and Obligations:

0 to $600 in monthly obligations	2
Over $600	1
Previous credit with this bank	4
Previous credit elsewhere	3
Checking account with this bank	2
Checking account elsewhere	1
Savings account with this bank	2
Savings account elsewhere	1
Telephone billed to applicant	2
Telephone billed to applicant's spouse	1

A loan officer will attempt to verify the information you provided by calling the telephone numbers you listed for your employer, landlord, etc. Assuming everything checks out, a good score on this system would be above 20 points. An unacceptable score would be below 12 points, and 13 to 19 points puts you in the gray area.

The thing that concerns most credit applicants is the loan officer's verification of information. Here is where I have some goodies for you. Keep the following in mind:

- Credit reviewers are human and have human qualities, including laziness.
- The loan officer is very busy and has dozens of applications to get through each day.
- The loan officer is expected to write a certain number of loans each week and needs to find goodcredit candidates even when few people are applyingfor credit.

- A loan officer may very well call your present employer and be happy to see that the phone number really exists and even happier if he is directed to your voice mail. (Remember Chapters 4 and 5?) Hearing this, most loan officers will assume you did not lie about your previous employer and will not bother to delve further.
- A busy loan officer may call your landlord and, upon hearing "You've reached Sunshine Apartments . . .," check off that box on your application and award you two points.

One time, a credit reviewer left two messages for me at my "place of business" (i.e., voice mail service). The message was, "I need to speak with Mr. Sheldon Charrett to verify his employment." At the time I was very busy and had enough credit, so I never bothered to call back. Nevertheless, two weeks later I had a credit card from that company. The credit reviewer, anxious to move on, apparently decided the valid phone number and voice mailbox was sufficient proof of my employment.

BE WARY OF MAIL DROPS

This book's original edition discussed how the major credit bureaus databased known mail drops and compared existing and newly established credit profiles to this database.

Obviously, with the new PMB rules (see Chapter 4), credit bureaus now have an even easier way to tell whether an address is actually a mail drop. If you think you need the credit points related to "residence," you may wish to employ other tactics discussed in Chapter 4.

CREDIT BUREAUS:
THE ULTIMATE PURVEYORS OF INFORMATION

Aside from the obvious advantages of establishing good credit with them, you can also use credit bureaus to obscure your existing identity through mutations. Sometimes a gradual mutation of your own identity can be a useful means of obtaining some minor privacy. The system's immense desire for information gathering renders it susceptible to the creative imagination of the identity changer.

I will use my own name and show how it has mutated over the years. The major credit bureaus have credit profiles on at least three of these mutations.

My name is Sheldon X. Charrett IV. When I was little, my parents called me Shelly, and as I got older people started calling me Shell (partly because of my name and partly because I didn't talk much). Of course, my teachers always called me Sheldon. Due to these quite innocent reasons, I have at various times been known as Sheldon X. Charrett IV, Sheldon X. Charrett Jr., Shelly Charrett, Shell Charrett, Shell X. Charrett, and Sheldon "Shell" Charrett.

Now add the mutations caused by error of various mailing list compilers and greedy credit card companies anxious to get me on their lists: Sheldon X. Charrette, Sheldon X. Charelle, Sheldon Charrett V, Shell Charet, Shelly Charnette, Sally Charrett, Shell Sharette, and Shell Charretti.

For most of my life I lived at 209 Heron Street in New Rochelle, New York. But over the years I have also received mail in my name for 299 Heron Street, 29 Heron Street, 20 Mount Heron Street, 209 Hermon Street, and 209 Harem Street.

All that was needed was to add one more thing to the soup: the filing of a mail forwarding card with the U.S. Postal Service. Information hounds love to research mail forwarding databases! List compilers deem themselves hot tortillas because they can track people down and keep mailing lists up to date.

From there it was a relatively simple matter to exploit the system's hunger for information and become Sherri Cheri with a wonderful credit history and a valid mailing address at a mom-and-pop Laundromat.

Of course you could extend this indefinitely by letting your already mutated identity continue to mutate, ramify, bifurcate, and otherwise live out the life of an amoebae, splitting into two, four, eight . . . well, you get the picture. The possibilities are astoundingly infinite. With careful planning and some research at your state's vital statistics registry, you can control the mutations so that your name just happens to have a birth certificate associated with it. All this happened through no real fault of your own. After all, is it up to you to quell the modern flow of information? Heck, all you wanted was a private mailbox and now you're someone else!

FINAL NOTES ON CREDIT

Credit grantors and credit bureaus are fairly powerful entities. As with any powerful adversary, the best approach is to use their power against them. They are big and bureaucratic and, therefore, fallible. There is no need to try and beat the credit bureaus at their game. The trick is to use their own game against them.

CHAPTER NINE

PI Tricks and Tips

When you make your living watching people who don't know they're being watched, it's hard not to learn a thing or two about the inner workings of the human mind. You also pick up a lot of tricks along the way that may or may not be interrelated—depending on your world perspective, that is. I tend to believe that, sooner or later, everything is connected to everything else. Eventually, somebody, somewhere, somehow, in some way is going to use the words "haiku" and "tuna fish sandwich" in the same sentence. See?

What follows are some comments, ideas, tips, tricks, and suggestions that find commonality in the life of an identity changer.

PART ONE: THE REALM OF THE TERMINALLY PARANOID

So you've done it. You're sitting in your new home, which is rented or titled to some person who doesn't really exist. You're free!

Or are you? You can no longer contact your family or friends. Boredom sets in. Your mind begins to wander as the Talking Heads are singing in the background, *This is not my beautiful house, this is not my beautiful wife!* You begin to wonder if the neighbors buy your story, if the landlord has contacted the FBI, if the lady down the hall is working undercover!

Just relax. This is only natural.

You've upset your whole lifestyle, your whole existence, and on top of that, you are in no position to "call up the guys" to go out and forget about life for a while.

There are plenty of things you can do to help yourself relax, regain control over your life, and alleviate the paranoia that may be setting in. If you believe that the lady down the hall is spying on you, then next time you see her, have a talk with her. You will know after a few minutes of casual conversation who she really is, and this will be one less thing for you to worry about. And what about that landlord? Well, his only concern is the rent, right? After all, he's not going to risk a vacancy by getting you thrown into a federal penitentiary. So, just pay your rent on time!

Besides, you'll never see the spies if they're any good at what they do. It's when you *don't* see spies—then you can get nervous.

Oops. I suppose that doesn't make you feel any better. Although I'm joking, there is an element of truth to what I say. If you think you spy a spy, you probably don't.

THE SPY GAME

The best way to gain confidence in your new surroundings is to achieve a better understanding of those surroundings. The way to rid yourself of the spy-demons that lurk in the shadows is to give them a taste of their own medicine. The best defense is a good offense. We can skirt the issue by using old clichés all night, but when it comes down to brass tacks, we're talking about spying back.

And you know what? You will feel a tremendous amount of relief when you find out that the neighbors couldn't care less about you. They are wrapped up in their own living, loving, and perhaps even some sociopathic activity of their own.

If you want to gather intelligence on your neighbors, two great resources are cordless phones and cellular phones. Many of your neighbors will have one or both of these marvels of modern technology, and the signals from both can be picked up on a handheld scanner. Thanks to the ECPA (Electronic Communications Privacy Act) of 1986, newer scanners won't receive cellular signals. You may want to search the used market for older scanners, which are either cellular capable or can be modified to become cellular capable.

Thanks also to the ECPA of 1986, the interception and monitoring of cellular telephone frequencies is illegal. Therefore you would only be purchasing or modifying a cellular-capable receiver in anticipation of the reversal of this insane law, right? Because as long as this law is in effect, you will be breaking it and subject to fines and/or imprisonment if you listen to cellular telephone conversations.

Conversely, there is currently no federal law prohibiting the interception and monitoring of cordless telephone conversations. However, various states and local districts, most notably California, have passed laws prohibiting the interception of any electronically transmitted signal. Therefore, you will need to check applicable state laws before intercepting any electronically transmitted communications. I trust that you will.

If you are not electronically literate, there are a few companies out there that specialize in the modification of cellular-capable receivers. Search out such companies on the World Wide Web.

While you're at it, you may also want to invest in a DTMF decoder. These little gadgets will decode any Touch-Tone phone beeps that happen to come in over your scanner. Companies that sell these can also be found out on the World Wide Web using such keywords as "DTMF," "scanner," and "modification."

NERVOUS ABOUT YOUR MAIL? TIME FOR SOME TEA!

Sooner or later you will receive a piece of mail that looks like it could be from a lawyer, bill collector, the IRS, jury duty, etc. If so, don't worry. Put the flame under the kettle and have a cup of tea!

It would be nice to find out the contents of the envelope without opening it, wouldn't it? That way, if you don't like the contents or if they seem to show that someone is on your trail, you can send the envelope back stamped "Addressee Unknown," "Addressee Moved," or whatever to throw them off your trail. To make it look official, I use postal lingo and a fast, bureaucratic pen stroke: AU RTS or UNK. RTS. Both mean "Addressee Unknown, Return to Sender" and is what the mailman would write. Then throw the letter in any corner mailbox and it will magically find its way back to the sender, who will assume it was never received or opened.

Obviously, you can't find out the contents without opening the envelope, so you'll have to do the next best thing: steam it open. Perhaps you've tried this before and became frustrated, thinking that steaming open mail was only something that television characters could do.

Fret not. It can be done, and done well. If you use the following procedure, you will have the envelope open in less than a minute without damaging the flap. In fact, the flap will still have enough good "glue" to seal it back up without anybody ever knowing. Here is the procedure.

Get a metal letter opener or a knife. By now the kettle should be boiling and whistling away. Shut off the flame. Clean the top of the kettle's spout with a damp dishcloth so that no dirt, grease, or grime is transferred onto the envelope.

Hold the envelope over the spout flap-side down so that the steam is evaporating right onto the lip of the flap and place your letter opener or knife into the flap. Gently slide it across the now-moist glue in a slight sawing motion. If done right, it should glide smoothly across the flap while opening it. Do not use any force, and do not leave the steam in any one area for too long or you'll melt away all the glue.

Remove the contents of the envelope, noting the exact arrangement of the enclosed materials so you can put everything back the same way (e.g., address must show through window if there is a window). If you find that someone is on your trail, stuff the letter back into the envelope and mark the envelope on the outside as described above. Be sure to not use your handwriting when you do this. One of those rubber stamp kits we discussed in Chapter 7 is handy for stamping envelopes as well as endorsing business checks. If there's not enough stick left on the flap, apply a few dabs of clear, fast-drying glue over the old stuff.

Drop the envelope in a mailbox in a different city or town so your local post office and mail carrier will not be confused by your denial of being at that address.

RESISTING TEMPTATIONS

A trick often used by bill collectors, investigators, and other nasty nosies is the old "send the sucker a check" routine. It works like this.

The investigator or bill collector, unable to find out where a particular subject does his or her banking, will send the subject a check made out by a bogus business. (Yes, they use them too!) A subject who is not street-smart may be tempted to deposit the check into his or her bank account. Big mistake! It will have been stamped by your bank when it was cleared. Bingo! When the investigator gets the check back, he now knows where he can attach assets and also has a better idea of where you are truly hanging out these days.

The best choice is to throw the check away. Some unscrupulous people I have known have "lost" these checks in poor neighborhoods so that they could be fraudulently cashed by homeless people or drug addicts, further throwing the investigator off the trail. Doing this, however, may be construed as assisting in a felony and could lead to criminal charges against you.

If you really want to cash the check, take it to the bank on which it is drawn. This really annoys investigators, as it causes them to lose money without gaining any additional information about their subject.

•➤

SAFE DRIVING METHODS FOR
THE TERMINALLY PARANOID

Whether you desire to live under a new identity or simply lead a private life, safe driving is of paramount importance. Why? Put simply, you don't want to attract the attention of police. Many people are hauled into court under criminal warrant or *capias* (civil arrest warrant). Most of these individuals never receive a knock on their door. The police depend on "catching" them during routine traffic stops. Once you are pulled over, they have the right to check Big Brother's data mines (National Crime Information Center, a/k/a NCIC, computer and standard local databases). If your name pops up or if something else is amiss (SSN seems inconsistent with given age, etc.), then the cops have a right to detain you for up to 48 hours without charging you with anything. During that 48 hours, they will investigate you and interrogate you to learn whatever information they can. This is not welcome attention for identity changers or privacy seekers, of course.

At red lights and stop signs, keep a car length between your front bumper and the vehicle in front of you. Be prepared to turn out to the left or right if someone comes running toward you with a flamethrower. Always have an escape route in mind.

Always know who is behind you on the highway or back roads. Pay attention to their movements. Are they trying too hard to stay a certain distance behind you? Do they appear to be talking to themselves? (If so, they may be speaking to their surveillance partner by radio.)

If you suspect you are being followed, use the following tactics to find out:

- Take three right turns. If the car you were suspicious of is still behind you, you are probably being followed.
- Go around a rotary twice. Again, if your tagalong made the same "mistake" you did, you are probably being followed.

- Pull over or go to a store. If the suspected vehicle also makes a pit stop, see what happens when you start driving again. If the other driver abruptly resumes his trip, you are probably being followed.

If you determine that you are in fact being followed, executing any of the following ideas will help temporarily throw someone off your trail:

- Drive right by your exit, street, apartment complex, or house (whichever applies).
- Go somewhere you've never gone before and act as if it's very important that you are there. Let your follower take a bunch of meaningless notes.
- Go "home" for the night to one of the larger motel chains. Pay the clerk and slip out the back. (Small, roadside motels don't have "backs" to slip out of—there is usually no way to leave your room other than in full view through the door by which you entered it.) If there appears to be no viable option to scram without the PI noticing, try using the pool, pretending to get ice from the ice machine, or spending some time in the rec hall, Jacuzzi, or lobby to throw him off. You could walk into town or go across the street to the convenient Chinese restaurant and make your getaway from there. Return for your vehicle after the PI has left.

Never drive while intoxicated. When you are driving, you are vulnerable. If you are drunk, you will eventually get cocky and make a mistake. Don't do it.

Let tailgaters pass you when it's appropriate to do so. This keeps you in the middle of the traffic stream, where you will stand out less to the authorities. Also, the speeders will keep the police busy if there should be any on the road ahead.

Conversely, if there is some reason you do not want a police car directly behind you, you may wish to keep the tailgater where he is. This way, when a police cruiser cuts out into traffic, he will be behind the tailgater instead of you.

Always register your vehicles to a mail drop in a company name (trust, corporation, etc.). By doing so, it will not lead somebody to your front door if they ever run your license plate.

PART TWO: DEALING WITH PAST CREDITORS

In the off chance that your reason for establishing a new identity is to avoid past creditors (gee, who would do a thing like that?), I will share with you some basic commandments that have helped my clients over the years. Although presented in the context of creditor evasion, these commandments are also invaluable in other identity changing endeavors.

KNOW THINE ENEMY

Creditors are like homing pigeons. If you have good credit, they will seek you out and solicit you perpetually until you apply for their preapproved credit card or take out a loan from their bank. After that, they'll solicit you just for the sake of soliciting you. Then, if you get stuck and can't pay, they will hound you until you fork over some cash that you probably don't have or have to get from another creditor.

But also know this: Banks and credit card companies are businesses, and business is all numbers. Creditors enter into all loans knowing full well that a certain percentage of these loans, usually 4 to 5 percent, will never be paid back. Thus, our creditor friends set up special departments or subsidiary corporations to deal with this 4 to 5 percent while the rest of the company happily goes about its business, raking in more money than you'll ever be able to imagine.

These collectors, as they are called, then endeavor to "recapture" some of the creditor's losses. They do this by calling up clients who have been unable to pay and encouraging them to make payments on their debt.

Any given bill collector sits behind a desk for eight hours a day making phone calls. They go right down their list making call after boring call. Some of the people they call are scared or feel guilty about their debt, and this makes the bill collector happy. He plays on this fear and guilt and gets the debtor to pay a portion of what they owe. The bill collector, in turn, is awarded a commission or other sales incentive as a result.

On the other hand, a small percentage of the people whom the collector calls never answer their phone or, if they do, are not scared or intimidated, nor do they feel guilty. Now tell me, is the collector going to spend a lot of time on these folks? Why should he? Every list of 100 debtors he receives has between 80 and 90 people on it who are willing to deal with him. He gets paid for getting money out of them. Do you honestly think he's going to waste time on the 10 or 20 folks who are obviously not interested in his services? It's a numbers game! So, a subcommandment here is: Thou Shalt Have An Answering Machine And Screen All Calls. If and when a creditor does catch you picking up the phone, under no circumstances should you indicate that you are even remotely willing to deal with him.

Of course, it is important to remember not to challenge or taunt the bill collector. If you make the situation personal, he may become motivated to make your life miserable. If you are caught picking up the phone, be professional and courteous. If it becomes necessary to hang up on the collector, do so as professionally as possible, without sarcasm or malice.

THOU SHALT NOT FILL OUT FORMS

Credit databases are intensely updated from various sources. It is vital that you understand that any form you file, check you sign, application you fill out, or magazine you subscribe to will lead creditors right to your door. This is true whether they want to lend you money or collect it from you.

Most people know that the information they fill out on any credit application will eventually end up in a computer. Fewer people know that these same computer databases are updated via mail forwarding and voter registration records. Very few people realize they are tracked through magazine subscriptions. Now that you are privy to this, you should conduct your affairs accordingly.

THOU SHALT BRAZENLY DEFEND THY RIGHTS

No matter how much you owe or what you did to get that far in debt, a bill collector must not invade your rights. Any time you feel your rights have been violated by a bill collector, write a letter to his superiors. If possible, cite the law that the bill collector has broken.

When the collection agency learns that you do not respond to phone calls and letters except to defend your rights, they will conclude that you are a bad risk. Not only will they never get anything out of you, but because you are educated and stand up for yourself, they expose themselves to liability by calling you. For a business, this is an untenable position.

Again, remember to maintain a firm, confident, businesslike manner. Engaging in a personal battle with a collector only opens the door to petty bureaucratic mischief—or worse. Your whole goal is to attract as little attention to yourself as possible.

SUMMARY

If you are scared, you are powerless. If you are always wondering when they are going to come and get you, your soul will wither away and your life of freedom will be meaningless.

By taking action and making the first move, you are placing yourself in a position of power and control. This is a much nicer way to live. Let the nasty nosies and the past creditors and investigators chase the scared and the guilt-ridden.

By believing in yourself, protecting your rights, and staying alert, you can ward off the jackals that would otherwise come crawling. Let them chase those who roll over and play dead. You are too intelligent for their game.

CHAPTER TEN

Going Home

⌣•

If you pull the big Houdini, you have to consider the possibility that one day you may wish to return home. Strictly speaking, if you're thinking about going home before you have even left, maybe you're not ready for this trip.

"Yeah, yeah, okay mom," I hear you saying, but, hey, this is reality. Think about it for a minute. Think back to all the other times you've left your home, either to go to school, take a trip, relocate for employment, or whatever. Is this any different? Well, yes. All those other times, you knew where your true home was and that you could go back anytime. But if you disappear and leave your whole life behind without so much as a word to your family and friends, there's a lot of finality.

This chapter highlights some of the more critical points of a complete disappearance.

WILL YOU BE DECLARED DEAD?

Most states have a statute where a person can be declared dead if no contact is made with that person after a specified period of time, say, seven years. In most cases, the spouse or immediate family must petition probate court in order for this to happen, as the courts will usually not act alone unless you owe the state money. If you have debts to the state and the state discovers abandoned assets belonging to you, it may petition probate court to declare you dead and have a public administrator settle your estate.

Other people to whom you are in debt may have you declared dead and proceed with action against your estate. This usually does not happen, as creditors often have no way of knowing your whereabouts unless the creditor was previously an acquaintance or knew your spouse or immediate family. In most cases, the creditor will assume you are hiding out in order to ditch your debts.

ABANDONED PROPERTY LAWS

Every state has a special office set up to handle unclaimed and abandoned property. This office is usually a division of either the state treasurer's office, the state comptroller's office, or the office of the receiver general. These are really three different terms that mean the same thing. The name of the division that handles unclaimed and abandoned property is usually the Abandoned Property Division or the Unclaimed Property Division.

All individuals residing in the state who have abandoned property on their books must turn the property over to the state for "safekeeping" within a certain statutory period. In most states the owner of abandoned property can claim it at any time. Certain states, most notably New Hampshire, place limits on the length of time that the true owner can assert his claim. Thus, you will serve yourself well to check the applicable state law.

Knowing this, you now have two things to think about:

- Protecting assets of a past identity
- Using the treasurer's office to hide money

The obvious solution to protecting assets of a past identity is not to leave any. Sometimes this may be unavoidable or undesirable, depending on your reasons for changing your identity. If for some reason you do have assets belonging to an identity that is on the lam, you may be able to just let those assets sit for years and years. The state may eventually take possession of them but, barring any laws to the contrary, you may someday be able to retrieve those assets, with interest.

When could you claim your abandoned assets? Well, if you are only disappearing temporarily, you can claim them upon your return "home." If you've changed your identity to hide from your family and the law is not after you, you can claim these assets at some point in the future and your family will never know about it.

If you've disappeared and are hiding from the law, you may have to give these assets up for good. If you're brazen enough, wait out the statute of limitations and then go back home to establish a claim. Provided you have properly researched the statute of limitations for whatever crime you've committed in the jurisdiction in which you committed it, you are safe. Make sure, however, that there is no other minor charge associated with the crime you committed that has a longer statute of limitations. If this is the case, the state or the feds will press that charge, and a judge will give you the maximum penalty even though the other crime was "forgotten."

For example, some states set a limiting statute of seven years for armed robbery. However, the federal statute for bank fraud is 10 years. So if you are stupid enough to try to rob banks for a living, don't assume that you are off the hook after eight years. A good prosecutor will argue that robbing a bank amounts to bank fraud, and the judge will send you away to nail you for the actual crime of armed robbery. Even though such a decision would probably get overturned in a higher court, you will be in jail for two to three years awaiting that trial.

The other useful thing about abandoned property laws is that you can use them backwards to hide money from creditors. Creditors never bother to think that their debtors may have abandoned property waiting for them, even if the creditor has a judgment against them. State departments of abandoned property do not bother to check for existing judgments prior to disbursing abandoned property proceeds.

If your state does not have a time limit (or if the time limit is long enough for your needs), the neat trick here is to have one of your "businesses" call the compliance division of the treasurer's office and request the form necessary for reporting abandoned property. Once you receive this form, fill it out, stating that the business has a $10,000 (or whatever) account payable to either yourself or some other business entity of which you have complete control. Send this form to the treasurer's office. A short time after this, the treasurer's office will write you stating that your business must send them a $10,000 check in order to establish an abandoned account for the person to whom the business is in debt (you). Send off the check. The treasurer's office will baby-sit your money for you while your creditors perform asset searches in bank account and real property databases. Many states will even pay interest on this money!

THE PROS AND CONS OF GOING ALONG WITH THE SYSTEM

There are those who read books such as this one in the hopes of avoiding civil or criminal prosecution. For example, clients have come to me looking to disappear in order to avoid a big lawsuit that had recently been slapped on them or to avoid an impending jail sentence.

In many such cases, it may be to your advantage to "go home," or never disappear in the first place. Of course, this depends on exactly who you've pissed off. If the impending matter is a civil lawsuit, you are probably better off seeing it through to the end. The worst thing that can happen in a civil suit is that you get a judgment against you. You will not be hauled off to jail that day. In fact, you will never be hauled off to jail as long as you do what the court says. The judge will not force you to pay more than you can afford.

In any case, if you see the civil matter through to the end, you will at least know what you're leaving behind should you decide to start a new life. Usually, civil lawsuits, even those involving fraud, can be settled through the courts and bankruptcy proceedings.

If you are expecting to be sued, then you'll want to go to the library and study up on bankruptcy prior to any attempt to hide or transfer your assets. There are several good books on the subject of dealing with creditors and surviving bankruptcy. In fact, I've read so many good books on the subject that it would be unfair to list only a few here. Go to the library. They are there.

Even if you are thinking about running away from a criminal proceeding against you, you may still be better off going along with the system. Things to consider:

- Offense committed
- Evidence against you
- State that is prosecuting you
- Plea bargains available
- Actual jail time you can expect to serve

Prison is not everything people say. If it were, there would not be so many repeat offenders. Prison systems are simply another institution run by the state. They are overcrowded, and as a result, most states have active work release, furlough, and house-arrest prison plans for nonviolent offenders. If you are not guilty of any violent offense, you will not be placed in the company of violent offenders, and you will probably not even see a prison that looks anything like what you've seen on television or in the movies. It'll probably look more like a hospital.

On the other hand, offenses such as first-degree murder, rape, and armed robbery are taken very seriously. People guilty of any of these offenses deserve to go to prison. The emotional scars left on the victims and the victims' families are irreparable. If such offenders are convicted, they will most likely be sent to a maximum security prison, more like what is portrayed on television.

CRIMES THAT GET LIGHTER SENTENCES

Believe it or not, even serious charges are often reduced to not-so-serious charges in plea bargains. In reality, courts are just too freakin' busy and love to move cases off the docket. Just agree to serve a little time so they can save face. In densely populated states, sentencing is surprisingly light, and actual jail time served is usually just enough to earn the offender a college degree. (This, of course, refers to nonviolent offenses. If you use violence or force in any escapade, you will hang, and rightly so.)

Financial crimes against banks and credit card companies are almost never prosecuted unless unusually large amounts of money are involved. The temptation of money is just too great. Banks are expected to reduce the temptation of fraud, and courts are typically not pleased with banks that leave themselves wide open to financial crimes. The courts and prisons are simply too busy with violent offenders to waste a lot of time on credit crooks. Even when prosecuted, sentences are usually suspended or, at most, extremely light.

Financial crimes against the elderly or otherwise unwitting investors are taken more seriously, and sentencing is harsher. Many sentences, though greater, are still suspended. However, repeat offenders will usually do jail time.

One of the best things to do if you are considering disappearing to avoid jail time is to check the sentencing guidelines for whatever offense it was that you committed. A lawyer, even a public defender, will usually know what kind of time you're looking at, based on these guidelines. It's also best to show up for every hearing and to not skip out on any trial dates (except for sentencing if you decide not to play along).

Why? I once had a client who was "on the run" for several years. He'd skipped trial right from the git-go. I asked him if he'd ever returned home to pull the court docket. He said no. I told him to have a family member pull the docket for him and read through it.

Turns out his public defender had the case summarily dismissed, even in his absence. The guy never needed to run away. He spent three years running from nothing. The public defender was busy and pissed at him for not showing up and so had no reason to try and track him down. It was onto the next case for him. I won't pretend to know how the public defender got the case dismissed without his client being present, but my guess is he pulled a fast one in a busy courtroom. Either the prosecution's representative was late, or they had lost evidence. Maybe he used my client as a bargaining chip for a more important case. Who knows?

The point? Never assume all hope is lost until the dimensionally challenged adult female croons gleefully (politically correct terminology for "fat lady sings").

SUMMARY

This chapter has highlighted some of the serious legal issues pertaining to an identity changer's return home. Obviously, anybody considering a complete identity change has issues to consider other than the legal implications mentioned in this chapter. Separating yourself from the emotional attachments you may have with your family and community is probably the biggest issue an identity changer has to consider. However, such personal and individual topics are not suitable for a book focused on changing your identity. Private issues such as whether a person can emotionally handle their own disappearance must be left to the individual considering such serious measures.

Conclusion

Identity documents are the tools of tyranny. Big Brother's ability to control our movements, track our whereabouts, and mold our habits allows for the production of die-cast citizens and the destruction of the individual.

When the masses allow their Social Security Numbers to be used as national identifiers, the bureaucratic machine is primed. When Corporate America keeps its employees close with rudimentary health care coverage and parsimonious pension plans, the gears of the machine are greased. When people preoccupy themselves with choosing between Coke and Pepsi, Burger King and McDonald's, or Republicans and Democrats, the machine is cranked and revving in high gear.

And thus the machine runs on.

But for every Winston Smith in the world who does not wish to become "6079 Smith W," there is a solution. Throw sand in the gears of that machine. Drain its grease and clog its fuel lines whenever possible. When you feel as though you've given more than enough and your privacy is on the line, run that machine in reverse for a while. Use it against itself. For you have one great advantage over the bureaucratic machine:

You can think.

And I suggest you do.

APPENDIX A

Social Security Number Area of Issue

The first three numbers of the SSN show where it was issued. Use this table as a quick reference to determine an SSN's area of issue. For example, any SSN beginning with 010 through 034 was issued in Massachusetts.

001–003	New Hampshire	247-251	South Carolina
004–007	Maine	654-658	
008–009	Vermont	252-260	Georgia
010–034	Massachusetts	667-675	
035–039	Rhode Island	261-267	Florida
040–049	Connecticut	589-595	
050–134	New York	766-772	
135–158	New Jersey	268-302	Ohio
159–211	Pennsylvania	303-317	Indiana
212–220	Maryland	318-361	Illinois
221–222	Delaware	362-386	Michigan
223–231	Virginia	387-399	Wisconsin
691–699 *		400-407	Kentucky
232–236	West Virginia	408-415	Tennessee
232	North Carolina	756-763 *	
237–246		416-424	Alabama
681–690			

425–428	Mississippi	526-527	Arizona
587–588 *		600-601	
752–755 *		764-765	
429–432	Arkansas	528-529	Utah
676–679		646-647	
433–439	Louisiana	530	Nevada
659–665		680	
440–448	Oklahoma	531-539	Washington
449–467	Texas	540-544	Oregon
627–645		545-573	California
468–477	Minnesota	602-626	
478–485	Iowa	574	Alaska
486–500	Missouri	575-576	Hawaii
501–502	North Dakota	750-751 *	
503–504	South Dakota	577-579	District of Columbia
505–508	Nebraska	580	Virgin Islands
509–515	Kansas	580-584	Puerto Rico
516–517	Montana	596-599	
518–519	Idaho	586	Guam
520	Wyoming	586	American Somoa
521–524	Colorado	586	Philippine Islands
650–653		700-728	Railroad Board **
525, 585	New Mexico	729-733 *	Enumeration at entry
648–649			

NOTE: The same area, when shown more than once, means that certain numbers have been transferred from one state to another, or that an area has been divided for use among certain geographic locations. Any number beginning with 000 will NEVER be a valid SSN.

* New areas allocated, but not yet issued.

** 700-728 Issuance of these numbers for railroad employees was discontinued July 1, 1963.

Appendix B

Highest Social Security Number Groups Issued

╰•

The Social Security Administration issues SSNs in groups. For example, the first group of Massachusetts SSNs issued was 010-01-xxxx. The SSA issues the groups in a certain order. First odd groups 01 through 09 are issued. Then even groups from 10 through 98. After they issue the last number from group 98, even groups from 02 though 08 are issued, followed by odd groups from 11 through 99. Because the SSA issues SSNs in a predictable pattern, you can often discover a fraudulent SSN if the middle digits indicate a group that has yet to be issued. Use this chart to determine the highest group issued for a given area.

The following chart was current as of 10/31/02. To check for updated information, go to:

http://www.ssa.gov/foia/highgroup.htm

001	98	002	96	003	96	004	04	005	04	006	02
007	02	008	86	009	86*	010	86	011	86	012	86
013	86	014	86	015	86	016	86	017	86	018	86
019	86	020	86*	021	84	022	84	023	84	024	84
025	84	026	84	027	84	028	84	029	84	030	84
031	84	032	84	033	84	034	84	035	68	036	68
037	68	038	68	039	68	040	04	041	04	042	04
043	04	044	04	045	04	046	04	047	04	048	04
049	02	050	92	051	92	052	92	053	92	054	92
055	92	056	92	057	92	058	92	059	92	060	92
061	92	062	92	063	92	064	92	065	92	066	92
067	92	068	92	069	92	070	92	071	92	072	92
073	92	074	92	075	92	076	92	077	92	078	92
079	92	080	92	081	92*	082	92*	083	92*	084	92*
085	90	086	90	087	90	088	90	089	90	090	90
091	90	092	90	093	90	094	90	095	90	096	90
097	90	098	90	099	90	100	90	101	90	102	90
103	90	104	90	105	90	106	90	107	90	108	90
109	90	110	90	111	90	112	90	113	90	114	90
115	90	116	90	117	90	118	90	119	90	120	90
121	90	122	90	123	90	124	90	125	90	126	90
127	90	128	90	129	90	130	90	131	90	132	90
133	90	134	90	135	11	136	11	137	11	138	11
139	11	140	11	141	11	142	11	143	11	144	11
145	11	146	11	147	11	148	11	149	11	150	11
151	11	152	11*	153	11*	154	08	155	08	156	08
157	08	158	08	159	80	160	80	161	80	162	80
163	80	164	80	165	80	166	80	167	80	168	80
169	80	170	80	171	80	172	80	173	80	174	80
175	80	176	80	177	80	178	80	179	80	180	80
181	80	182	80	183	80	184	80	185	80	186	80
187	80	188	80	189	80	190	80	191	80	192	80

193	80	194	80	195	80	196	80	197	80*	198	80*
199	78	200	78	201	78	202	78	203	78	204	78
205	78	206	78	207	78	208	78	209	78	210	78
211	78	212	65	213	65	214	65	215	65*	216	63
217	63	218	63	219	63	220	63	221	96	222	94
223	95	224	95	225	95*	226	93	227	93	228	93
229	93	230	93	231	93	232	49	233	49	234	49
235	49	236	47	237	99	238	99	239	99	240	99
241	99	242	99	243	99	244	99	245	99	246	99*
247	99	248	99	249	99	250	99	251	99	252	99
253	99	254	99	255	99	256	99	257	99	258	99
259	99	260	99	261	99	262	99	263	99	264	99
265	99	266	99	267	99	268	08	269	08	270	08*
271	08*	272	06	273	06	274	06	275	06	276	06
277	06	278	06	279	06	280	06	281	06	282	06
283	06	284	06	285	06	286	06	287	06	288	06
289	06	290	06	291	06	292	06	293	06	294	06
295	06	296	06	297	06	298	06	299	06	300	06
301	06	302	06	303	25	304	25	305	25	306	25
307	25	308	25	309	25	310	25	311	25	312	25
313	25	314	25	315	25*	316	23	317	23	318	02
319	02	320	02	321	02	322	02	323	02	324	02
325	02	326	02*	327	02*	328	98	329	98	330	98
331	98	332	98	333	98	334	98	335	98	336	98
337	98	338	98	339	98	340	98	341	98	342	98
343	98	344	98	345	98	346	98	347	98	348	98
349	98	350	98	351	98	352	98	353	98	354	98
355	98	356	98	357	98	358	98	359	98	360	98
361	98	362	29	363	29*	364	29*	365	27	366	27
367	27	368	27	369	27	370	27	371	27	372	27
373	27	374	27	375	27	376	27	377	27	378	27
379	27	380	27	381	27	382	27	383	27	384	27

385	27	386	27	387	23	388	23	389	23	390	23
391	23	392	21	393	23*	394	21	395	21	396	21
397	21	398	21	399	21	400	59	401	59	402	59
403	59	404	59	405	59	406	57	407	57	408	93
409	93	410	93	411	93	412	93	413	93	414	93
415	93*	416	55	417	55	418	55	419	53	420	53
421	53	422	53	423	53	424	53	425	93	426	91
427	91	428	91	429	99	430	99	431	99	432	99
433	99	434	99	435	99	436	99	437	99	438	99
439	99	440	17	441	17	442	17	443	17	444	17*
445	15	446	15	447	15	448	15	449	99	450	99
451	99	452	99	453	99	454	99	455	99	456	99
457	99	458	99	459	99	460	99	461	99	462	99
463	99	464	99	465	99	466	99	467	99	468	41
469	41	470	41	471	41	472	41	473	41	474	41
475	41	476	41*	477	39	478	33	479	33*	480	31
481	31	482	31	483	31	484	31	485	31	486	19
487	19	488	19	489	19	490	19	491	19	492	19
493	19	494	19	495	19	496	19	497	19*	498	17
499	17	500	17	501	29	502	27	503	33	504	33
505	45	506	45	507	45*	508	43	509	21	510	21
511	21	512	21	513	21	514	19	515	19	516	37
517	37	518	65	519	63	520	45	521	99	522	99
523	99	524	99	525	99	526	99	527	99	528	99
529	99	530	99	531	51	532	51	533	51*	534	49
535	49	536	49	537	49	538	49	539	49	540	63
541	63	542	63	543	61	544	61	545	99	546	99
547	99	548	99	549	99	550	99	551	99	552	99
553	99	554	99	555	99	556	99	557	99	558	99
559	99	560	99	561	99	562	99	563	99	564	99
565	99	566	99	567	99	568	99	569	99	570	99
571	99	572	99	573	99	574	37*	575	95	576	93

577	35*	578	33	579	33	580	35	581	99	582	99
583	99	584	99	585	99	586	49	587	91	589	99
590	99	591	99	592	99	593	99	594	99	595	99
596	72*	597	70	598	70	599	70	600	99	601	99
602	35	603	35	604	35	605	35	606	35	607	35
608	35	609	35	610	35	611	35*	612	35*	613	35*
614	35*	615	35*	616	35*	617	35*	618	35*	619	35*
620	33	621	33	622	33	623	33	624	33	625	33
626	33	627	84	628	84*	629	84*	630	84*	631	84*
632	82	633	82	634	82	635	82	636	82	637	82
638	82	639	82	640	82	641	82	642	82	643	82
644	82	645	82	646	68*	647	66	648	28	649	28
650	24	651	24	652	24	653	24*	654	14	655	14*
656	12	657	12	658	12	659	07	660	05	661	05
662	05	663	05	664	05	665	05	667	16	668	16
669	16	670	16	671	16	672	16	673	16*	674	14
675	14	676	03	677	03	678	03	679	03	680	44*
681	01*	700	18	701	18	702	18	703	18	704	18
705	18	706	18	707	18	708	18	709	18	710	18
711	18	712	18	713	18	714	18	715	18	716	18
717	18	718	18	719	18	720	18	721	18	722	18
723	18	724	28	725	18	726	18	727	10	728	14
764	24	765	24*	766	14	767	14	768	14	769	14
770	14*	771	14*	772	14*						

APPENDIX C

Geographic and Chronological Distribution of Social Security Numbers

᎑•

As you'll recall from Appendix B, the Social Security Administration issues SSNs in groupings enumerated by the middle digits. You'll also recall that the SSA issues these groups in a very specific pattern. By knowing this pattern and keeping track of when the highest group changes in a given area, one can compile a listing of which year the SSA issued a given group in a given area. Banks and credit reporting agencies have done this over the years, as has the SSA. This appendix is such a listing. It is the most complete one I have at the time of this writing. It is valid for all states for the years 1951 through 1978.

STATE	Area	1951	1952	1953	1954	1955	1956	1957	1958	1959	1960	1961	1962	1963	1964	1965	1966	1967	1968	1969	1970	1971	1972	1973	1974	1975	1976	1977	78
NH	001	26	26	28	28	28	30	32	32	32	32	34	36	36	38	40	42	42	44	46	46	48	48	54	56	56	58	60	60
NH	002	26	26	26	28	28	30	30	30	32	32	34	34	38	38	40	40	42	44	44	46	46	48	52	54	56	58	60	60
NH	003	24	26	26	26	28	28	30	30	32	32	32	34	38	38	38	40	42	42	44	46	46	48	52	54	56	58	58	58
ME	004	32	34	36	36	38	40	40	40	42	42	44	46	50	50	50	52	54	56	56	58	60	62	66	68	70	72	72	74
ME	005	32	34	34	36	38	40	40	40	42	42	44	44	48	50	50	52	54	54	56	58	60	62	64	66	68	70	72	72
ME	006	32	34	34	34	36	38	40	40	40	42	44	44	48	48	50	52	54	54	56	58	60	62	64	66	68	70	72	72
ME	007	32	32	34	34	36	38	38	40	40	42	42	44	46	48	50	50	52	54	56	58	58	60	64	66	68	70	70	72
VT	008	24	24	26	26	28	28	28	30	30	32	32	34	36	36	38	40	40	42	42	44	46	46	54	54	58	60	60	60
VT	009	22	24	24	24	26	28	28	28	30	30	32	32	34	36	38	38	40	40	42	44	46	52	54	56	58	58	58	58
MA	010	28	28	28	30	30	30	32	32	32	34	34	36	38	38	40	42	42	44	46	46	48	48	50	52	54	54	58	58
MA	011	26	28	28	30	30	30	32	32	32	34	34	36	38	38	40	42	42	44	46	46	48	48	50	52	54	54	58	58
MA	012	26	28	28	28	28	30	32	32	32	34	34	36	38	38	40	42	42	44	46	46	48	48	50	52	54	54	58	58
MA	013	28	28	28	28	30	30	32	32	32	34	34	36	38	38	40	42	42	44	44	46	48	48	50	52	54	54	58	58
MA	014	26	28	28	28	30	30	32	32	32	34	34	36	38	38	40	42	44	46	46	46	48	48	50	52	54	54	56	58
MA	015	26	28	28	28	30	30	30	32	32	34	34	34	38	38	40	42	42	44	44	46	48	48	50	52	54	54	56	58
MA	016	28	28	28	28	30	30	30	32	32	32	34	34	38	38	40	42	44	46	46	48	48	50	52	54	54	56	58	58
MA	017	26	28	28	28	30	30	32	32	32	34	34	36	38	38	40	42	44	44	46	48	48	50	52	54	54	56	58	58
MA	018	26	28	28	28	30	30	30	32	32	35	34	34	38	40	42	44	44	46	46	48	48	50	52	54	54	56	58	58
MA	019	26	28	28	28	30	30	30	32	32	32	34	34	38	40	42	44	44	46	46	48	48	50	52	54	54	56	58	58
MA	020	26	28	28	28	30	30	30	32	32	32	34	34	36	38	40	40	42	44	44	46	48	48	50	52	52	54	56	58
MA	021	26	28	28	28	30	30	30	32	32	32	34	34	36	38	40	40	42	44	44	46	48	48	50	52	52	54	56	58
MA	022	26	26	28	28	30	30	30	30	32	32	34	34	38	38	40	40	42	44	44	46	48	48	50	52	52	54	56	58
MA	023	26	26	28	28	28	30	30	30	32	32	34	34	38	40	40	42	42	44	46	48	48	50	52	52	54	56	58	58
MA	024	26	26	28	28	28	30	30	30	32	32	34	34	36	38	38	40	42	42	44	46	48	48	50	52	52	54	56	58
MA	025	26	26	28	28	28	30	30	30	32	32	34	34	36	38	38	40	42	44	46	46	48	48	50	52	52	54	56	58
MA	026	26	26	28	28	28	30	30	30	32	32	34	34	36	38	38	40	42	42	44	46	46	48	50	52	52	54	56	58
MA	027	26	26	28	28	28	30	30	30	32	32	32	34	36	38	38	40	42	42	44	46	46	48	50	52	52	54	56	58
MA	028	26	26	28	28	28	30	30	30	32	32	32	34	36	38	38	40	40	42	44	46	46	48	50	52	52	54	56	58
MA	029	26	26	28	28	28	30	30	30	32	32	32	34	36	38	38	40	42	44	46	48	50	50	52	54	56	56		
MA	030	26	26	28	28	28	30	30	30	32	32	32	34	36	38	38	40	42	42	44	46	46	48	50	50	52	54	56	56
MA	031	26	26	28	28	28	30	30	30	32	32	34	36	38	38	40	42	42	44	44	46	48	50	50	52	54	56	56	
MA	032	26	26	28	28	28	28	30	30	30	32	32	34	36	38	38	40	42	42	44	44	46	48	50	50	52	54	56	56
MA	033	26	26	28	28	28	28	30	30	30	32	32	34	36	38	38	40	42	42	44	44	46	48	50	50	52	54	56	56
MA	034	26	26	28	28	28	28	30	30	30	32	32	34	36	36	38	40	42	42	44	46	46	50	50	52	52	54	56	56
RI	035	22	24	24	26	26	26	26	26	28	28	28	30	32	32	32	34	36	36	38	38	38	40	42	44	46	46	48	48
RI	036	22	24	24	24	24	26	26	26	26	28	28	30	32	32	32	32	34	34	36	36	38	38	40	42	44	44	46	48	48

STATE	Area	1951	1952	1953	1954	1955	1956	1957	1958	1959	1960	1961	1962	1963	1964	1965	1966	1967	1968	1969	1970	1971	1972	1973	1974	1975	1976	1977	78
RI	037	22	22	24	24	24	26	26	26	26	28	28	28	30	32	32	34	34	36	36	38	38	40	42	44	44	46	46	46
RI	038	22	22	24	24	24	24	26	26	28	28	28	28	30	30	32	32	34	34	36	36	38	38	42	42	44	44	46	46
RI	039	22	22	24	24	24	24	24	26	26	26	26	28	30	30	32	32	34	34	36	36	38	38	42	42	44	44	46	46
CT	040	28	28	30	30	30	32	32	34	34	34	36	38	42	42	44	46	48	48	50	52	54	56	60	62	64	68	68	68
CT	041	26	28	30	30	30	32	32	34	34	34	36	38	40	42	44	46	48	48	50	52	54	56	60	62	64	66	68	68
CT	042	26	28	30	30	30	32	32	34	34	34	36	38	40	42	44	46	46	48	50	52	54	54	60	62	64	66	68	68
CT	043	26	28	30	30	30	30	32	34	34	34	36	38	40	42	42	44	46	48	50	52	54	54	60	62	64	66	68	68
CT	044	26	28	28	30	30	30	32	32	34	34	36	40	42	44	44	46	48	50	52	54	54	60	62	64	66	66	66	68
CT	045	26	28	28	30	30	30	32	32	34	34	36	40	42	44	44	46	48	50	52	52	54	60	62	64	66	66	66	68
CT	046	26	28	28	30	30	30	32	32	32	34	34	36	40	40	42	44	46	48	50	52	52	54	58	60	64	66	66	68
CT	047	26	26	28	30	30	30	30	32	32	34	34	36	38	40	42	44	46	48	48	50	52	54	58	60	64	66	66	66
CT	048	26	28	28	30	30	30	30	32	32	34	34	36	38	40	42	44	46	48	50	50	52	54	58	60	62	66	66	66
CT	049	26	26	28	28	28	30	30	32	32	34	34	36	38	40	42	44	46	46	48	50	52	54	58	60	62	66	66	66
NY	050	28	28	30	30	30	32	32	34	34	34	36	36	38	40	42	42	44	46	46	48	50	50	54	54	56	60	60	62
NY	051	28	28	30	30	30	32	32	34	34	34	36	36	40	40	42	42	44	46	46	46	50	50	54	54	56	60	60	62
NY	052	28	28	30	30	30	32	32	34	34	34	36	36	40	40	42	42	44	46	46	48	50	50	54	54	56	60	60	62
NY	053	28	28	30	30	30	32	32	34	34	34	36	36	40	40	42	42	44	46	46	48	50	50	54	54	56	60	60	62
NY	054	28	28	30	30	30	32	32	34	34	34	36	36	40	40	42	42	44	46	46	48	50	50	54	54	56	60	60	62
NY	055	28	28	30	30	30	32	32	34	34	34	36	36	40	40	42	42	44	46	46	48	50	50	54	54	56	58	60	62
NY	056	28	28	30	30	30	32	32	34	34	34	36	36	40	40	42	42	44	46	46	48	50	50	54	54	56	58	60	62
NY	057	28	28	30	30	30	32	32	34	34	34	36	36	40	40	42	42	44	46	46	48	50	50	54	54	56	58	60	62
NY	058	28	28	30	30	30	32	32	34	34	34	36	36	40	40	42	42	44	44	46	48	50	50	54	54	56	58	60	62
NY	059	28	28	30	30	30	32	32	32	34	34	36	36	40	40	42	42	44	46	46	48	50	50	54	54	56	58	60	62
NY	060	28	28	30	30	30	32	32	34	34	34	36	36	40	40	42	42	44	46	46	48	50	50	54	54	56	58	60	62
NY	061	28	28	30	30	30	32	32	34	34	34	36	36	40	40	42	42	44	46	46	48	50	50	54	54	56	58	60	62
NY	062	28	28	30	30	30	32	32	34	34	34	36	36	40	40	42	42	44	46	46	48	50	50	54	54	56	58	60	62
NY	063	28	28	30	30	30	32	32	34	34	34	36	36	40	40	42	42	44	46	46	48	50	50	54	54	56	58	60	62
NY	064	28	28	30	30	30	32	32	34	34	34	36	36	40	40	42	42	44	46	46	48	50	50	52	54	56	58	60	62
NY	065	28	28	30	30	30	32	32	34	34	34	36	36	40	40	42	42	44	44	46	48	50	50	52	54	56	58	60	62
NY	066	28	28	30	30	30	32	32	34	34	34	36	36	40	40	40	42	44	44	46	48	50	50	52	54	56	58	60	62
NY	067	28	28	30	30	30	32	32	32	34	34	36	36	40	40	40	42	44	44	46	48	50	50	52	54	56	58	60	62
NY	068	28	28	30	30	30	32	32	34	34	34	36	36	40	40	40	42	44	44	46	48	50	50	52	54	56	58	60	62
NY	069	28	28	28	30	30	32	32	32	34	34	36	36	40	40	40	42	44	44	46	48	50	50	52	54	56	58	60	62
NY	070	28	28	30	30	30	32	32	32	34	34	36	36	40	40	40	42	44	46	46	48	50	50	52	54	56	58	60	62
NY	071	28	28	30	30	30	32	32	34	34	34	36	36	40	40	40	42	44	44	46	48	50	50	52	54	56	58	60	62
NY	072	28	28	28	30	30	32	32	32	34	34	36	36	40	40	40	42	44	46	46	48	50	50	52	54	56	58	60	62
NY	073	28	28	28	30	30	32	32	32	34	34	36	36	40	40	40	42	44	44	46	48	50	50	52	54	56	58	60	62
NY	074	28	28	28	30	30	32	32	32	34	34	36	36	40	40	40	42	44	44	46	48	50	50	52	54	56	58	60	62

STATE	Area	1951	1952	1953	1954	1955	1956	1957	1958	1959	1960	1961	1962	1963	1964	1965	1966	1967	1968	1969	1970	1971	1972	1973	1974	1975	1976	1977	78
NY	075	28	28	28	30	30	32	32	32	34	34	36	36	40	40	40	42	44	44	46	48	50	50	52	54	56	58	60	62
NY	076	28	28	28	30	30	32	32	32	34	34	36	36	38	40	40	42	44	44	46	48	50	52	52	54	56	58	60	62
NY	077	26	28	28	30	30	32	32	32	34	34	34	36	38	40	40	42	44	44	46	48	50	52	52	54	56	58	60	62
NY	078	26	28	28	28	30	32	32	32	34	34	34	36	38	40	40	42	44	44	46	48	50	52	52	54	56	58	60	62
NY	079	28	28	28	30	30	32	32	32	34	34	36	36	38	40	40	42	44	44	46	48	50	52	52	54	56	58	60	62
NY	080	26	28	28	30	30	32	32	32	34	34	34	36	38	40	40	42	44	44	46	48	50	52	52	54	56	58	60	62
NY	081	28	28	28	30	30	32	32	32	34	34	36	38	40	40	40	42	44	44	46	48	50	52	52	54	56	58	60	62
NY	082	26	28	28	30	30	30	32	32	34	34	34	36	38	40	40	42	44	44	46	48	50	52	52	54	56	58	60	60
NY	083	26	28	28	30	30	30	32	32	34	34	34	36	38	40	40	42	44	44	46	48	50	52	52	54	56	58	60	60
NY	084	26	28	28	30	30	30	32	32	34	34	34	36	38	40	40	42	44	44	46	48	50	52	52	54	56	58	60	60
NY	085	26	28	28	30	30	30	32	32	34	34	34	36	38	40	40	42	44	44	46	48	50	52	52	54	56	58	60	60
NY	086	28	28	28	30	30	30	32	32	34	34	34	36	38	40	40	42	44	44	46	48	50	52	52	54	56	58	60	60
NY	087	28	28	28	30	30	30	32	32	34	34	34	36	38	40	40	42	44	44	46	48	50	52	52	54	56	58	60	60
NY	088	28	28	28	30	30	30	32	32	34	34	34	36	38	40	40	42	44	44	46	48	50	52	52	54	56	58	60	60
NY	089	26	28	28	30	30	30	32	32	34	34	34	36	38	40	40	42	44	44	46	48	50	52	52	54	56	58	60	60
NY	090	28	28	28	30	30	30	32	32	34	34	34	36	38	40	40	42	44	44	46	48	50	52	52	54	56	58	60	60
NY	091	26	28	28	30	30	30	32	32	34	34	34	36	38	40	40	42	42	44	46	48	50	52	52	54	56	58	60	60
NY	092	26	28	28	30	30	30	32	32	34	34	34	36	38	40	40	42	44	44	46	48	50	52	52	54	56	58	60	60
NY	093	26	28	28	30	30	30	32	32	34	34	34	36	38	40	40	42	42	44	46	48	50	52	52	54	56	58	60	60
NY	094	26	28	28	30	30	30	32	32	34	34	34	36	38	40	40	42	44	44	46	48	50	52	52	54	56	58	60	60
NY	095	26	28	28	30	30	30	32	32	34	34	34	36	38	38	40	42	44	44	46	48	50	52	52	54	56	58	60	60
NY	096	26	28	28	30	30	30	32	32	34	34	34	36	38	40	40	42	42	44	46	48	50	52	52	54	56	58	60	60
NY	097	26	28	28	30	30	30	32	32	34	34	34	36	38	38	40	42	44	44	46	48	50	52	52	54	56	58	60	60
NY	098	26	28	28	30	30	30	32	32	34	34	34	36	38	38	40	42	44	44	46	48	50	52	52	54	56	58	60	60
NY	099	26	28	28	30	30	30	32	32	32	34	34	36	38	40	40	42	42	44	46	48	50	52	52	54	56	58	60	60
NY	100	26	28	28	30	30	30	32	32	32	34	34	36	38	38	40	42	42	44	46	48	50	52	52	54	56	58	60	60
NY	101	26	28	28	30	30	30	32	32	32	34	34	36	38	38	40	40	42	44	46	46	48	50	52	54	56	58	60	60
NY	102	26	28	28	28	30	30	32	32	32	34	34	36	38	38	40	40	42	44	46	46	48	50	52	54	56	58	60	60
NY	103	26	28	28	28	30	30	32	32	32	34	34	36	38	38	40	40	42	44	46	46	48	50	52	54	56	58	60	60
NY	104	26	28	28	28	30	30	32	32	32	34	34	36	38	38	40	40	42	44	46	48	48	50	52	54	56	58	60	60
NY	105	26	28	28	28	30	30	32	32	32	34	34	36	38	38	40	40	42	44	46	48	48	50	52	54	56	58	60	60
NY	106	26	28	28	28	30	30	32	32	32	34	34	36	38	38	40	40	42	44	46	46	48	50	52	54	56	58	60	60
NY	107	26	28	28	28	30	30	32	32	32	34	34	36	38	38	40	40	42	44	46	46	48	50	52	54	56	58	60	60
NY	108	26	28	28	28	30	30	32	32	32	34	34	36	38	38	40	40	42	44	46	46	48	50	52	54	56	58	60	60
NY	109	26	28	28	28	30	30	32	32	32	34	34	36	38	38	40	40	42	44	46	46	48	50	52	54	56	58	60	60
NY	110	26	28	28	28	30	30	32	32	32	34	34	36	38	38	40	40	42	44	46	46	48	50	52	54	56	58	60	60
NY	111	26	28	28	28	30	30	32	32	32	34	34	36	38	38	40	40	42	44	46	46	48	50	52	54	56	58	60	60
NY	112	26	28	28	28	30	30	32	32	32	34	34	36	38	38	40	40	42	44	46	46	48	50	52	54	56	58	60	60
NY	113	26	28	28	28	30	30	30	32	32	34	34	36	38	38	40	40	42	44	46	46	48	50	52	54	56	58	60	60
NY	114	26	28	28	28	30	30	30	32	32	32	34	36	38	38	40	40	42	44	46	48	48	50	52	54	56	58	60	60

STATE	Area	1951	1952	1953	1954	1955	1956	1957	1958	1959	1960	1961	1962	1963	1964	1965	1966	1967	1968	1969	1970	1971	1972	1973	1974	1975	1976	1977	78
NY	115	26	28	28	28	30	30	32	32	32	34	34	36	38	38	40	40	42	44	46	48	48	50	52	54	56	58	60	60
NY	116	26	28	28	28	30	30	30	32	32	34	34	36	38	38	40	40	42	44	46	46	48	50	52	54	56	58	60	60
NY	117	26	28	28	28	30	30	32	32	32	34	34	36	38	38	40	40	42	44	46	48	48	50	52	54	56	58	60	60
NY	118	26	28	28	28	30	30	32	32	32	34	34	36	38	38	40	40	42	44	46	46	48	50	52	54	56	58	60	60
NY	119	26	28	28	28	30	30	32	32	32	34	34	36	38	38	40	40	42	44	46	46	48	50	52	54	56	58	60	60
NY	120	26	28	28	28	30	30	32	32	32	34	34	36	38	38	40	40	42	44	46	46	48	50	52	54	56	58	60	60
NY	121	26	28	28	28	30	30	32	32	32	34	34	36	38	38	40	40	42	44	46	46	48	50	52	54	56	58	60	60
NY	122	26	26	28	28	30	30	32	32	32	34	34	36	38	38	40	40	42	44	46	46	48	50	52	54	56	58	58	60
NY	123	26	26	28	28	30	30	32	32	32	34	34	36	38	38	40	40	42	44	46	46	48	50	52	54	56	58	58	60
NY	124	26	26	28	28	30	30	30	32	32	34	34	36	38	38	40	40	42	44	46	46	48	50	52	54	56	58	58	60
NY	125	26	26	28	28	30	30	32	32	32	34	34	34	38	38	40	40	42	44	46	46	48	50	52	54	56	58	58	60
NY	126	26	26	28	28	30	30	30	32	32	34	34	34	38	38	40	40	42	44	44	46	50	52	54	54	54	58	58	60
NY	127	26	26	28	28	30	30	30	32	32	34	34	34	38	38	40	40	42	44	44	46	50	52	54	54	54	58	58	60
NY	128	26	26	28	28	30	30	30	32	32	34	34	34	38	40	40	40	42	44	44	46	50	52	54	54	54	58	58	60
NY	129	26	26	28	28	30	30	30	32	32	34	34	34	38	40	40	40	42	44	44	46	50	52	54	54	54	58	58	60
NY	130	26	26	28	28	30	30	30	32	32	34	34	34	38	40	40	42	44	44	46	50	52	54	54	54	58	58	60
NY	131	26	26	28	28	30	30	30	32	32	34	34	34	38	38	40	40	42	44	46	46	50	52	52	52	54	58	58	60
NY	132	26	26	28	28	30	30	30	32	32	32	34	34	36	38	40	40	42	44	44	46	50	52	52	52	54	58	58	60
NY	133	26	26	28	28	30	30	30	32	32	32	34	34	36	38	38	40	40	42	44	44	46	50	52	52	52	54	58	58	60
NY	134	26	26	28	28	30	30	30	32	34	34	34	34	36	38	40	40	42	44	44	46	48	52	52	52	54	58	58	60
NJ	135	26	28	28	30	30	32	32	32	34	34	36	36	38	40	42	44	46	46	48	50	52	56	58	58	62	64	66	68
NJ	136	26	28	28	30	30	32	32	32	34	34	36	36	38	40	42	44	46	46	48	50	52	56	58	58	62	64	66	68
NJ	137	26	28	28	30	30	30	32	32	34	34	36	36	40	40	42	44	46	46	48	50	52	56	58	58	62	64	66	68
NJ	138	26	28	28	28	30	30	32	32	34	34	36	36	38	40	42	44	44	46	48	50	52	56	58	58	62	64	66	68
NJ	139	26	28	28	28	30	30	32	32	34	34	34	36	38	40	42	44	44	46	48	50	52	56	58	58	62	64	66	68
NJ	140	26	28	28	28	30	30	32	32	34	34	36	38	40	42	44	44	46	48	50	52	56	58	58	60	64	66	68
NJ	141	26	28	28	28	30	30	32	32	34	34	36	38	40	42	44	44	46	48	50	52	56	58	58	60	64	66	68
NJ	142	26	28	28	28	30	30	32	32	32	34	34	36	38	40	42	42	44	46	48	50	52	56	58	58	60	64	66	68
NJ	143	26	28	28	28	30	30	32	32	32	34	34	36	38	40	42	42	44	46	48	50	52	56	58	58	60	64	66	66
NJ	144	26	26	28	28	30	30	32	32	32	34	34	36	38	40	42	42	44	46	48	50	52	56	58	58	60	64	66	66
NJ	145	26	26	28	28	30	30	32	32	32	34	34	36	38	40	40	42	44	46	48	50	52	56	58	58	60	64	66	66
NJ	146	26	26	28	28	30	30	32	32	32	34	34	36	38	40	40	42	44	46	48	50	52	56	58	58	60	64	66	66
NJ	147	26	26	28	28	30	30	32	32	32	34	34	38	40	40	42	44	46	48	48	52	56	58	58	60	62	66	66
NJ	148	26	26	28	28	30	30	32	32	32	34	34	36	38	40	40	42	44	46	48	50	52	56	58	58	60	62	66	66
NJ	149	26	26	28	28	30	30	30	32	32	34	34	36	38	40	40	42	44	46	48	48	52	56	58	58	60	62	66	66
NJ	150	26	26	28	28	30	30	30	32	32	34	34	36	38	40	40	42	44	46	48	48	52	56	58	58	60	62	66	66
NJ	151	26	26	28	28	28	30	30	32	32	34	34	36	38	38	40	42	44	46	46	48	50	52	56	58	60	62	64	66
NJ	152	26	26	28	28	28	30	30	32	32	34	34	36	38	38	40	42	44	46	46	48	50	52	56	58	60	62	64	66
NJ	153	26	26	28	28	28	30	30	32	32	34	34	38	38	40	42	44	46	48	48	50	52	54	58	60	62	64	66

STATE	Area	1951	1952	1953	1954	1955	1956	1957	1958	1959	1960	1961	1962	1963	1964	1965	1966	1967	1968	1969	1970	1971	1972	1973	1974	1975	1976	1977	78
NJ	154	24	26	26	28	28	30	30	32	32	32	34	34	38	38	40	42	44	46	48	48	50	52	54	58	60	62	64	66
NJ	155	24	26	26	28	28	30	30	32	32	32	34	34	38	38	40	42	44	46	46	48	50	52	54	58	60	62	64	66
NJ	156	26	26	26	28	28	30	30	32	32	32	34	34	38	38	40	42	44	44	46	48	50	52	54	58	60	62	64	66
NJ	157	26	26	26	28	28	30	30	30	32	32	34	34	38	38	40	42	44	44	46	48	50	52	54	58	60	62	64	66
NJ	158	26	26	26	28	28	30	30	32	32	32	34	34	38	38	40	42	44	44	46	48	50	52	54	56	60	62	64	66
PA	159	28	28	30	30	30	32	32	34	34	34	36	36	38	40	40	42	44	44	46	46	48	48	52	52	54	56	58	58
PA	160	28	28	30	30	30	32	32	34	34	34	36	36	38	40	40	42	44	44	46	46	48	48	52	52	54	56	58	58
PA	161	28	28	30	30	30	32	32	34	34	34	36	36	38	40	40	42	42	44	46	46	48	48	52	52	54	56	58	58
PA	162	28	28	30	30	30	32	32	34	34	34	36	36	38	40	40	42	42	44	46	46	48	48	52	52	54	56	58	58
PA	163	28	28	30	30	30	32	32	34	34	34	36	36	38	40	40	42	42	44	46	46	48	48	52	52	54	56	58	58
PA	164	28	28	30	30	30	32	32	34	34	34	36	36	38	40	40	42	42	44	46	46	48	48	52	52	54	56	58	58
PA	165	28	28	30	30	30	32	32	32	34	34	34	36	38	38	40	42	42	44	46	46	48	48	52	52	54	56	58	58
PA	166	28	28	30	30	30	32	32	32	34	34	36	36	38	38	40	42	42	44	46	46	48	48	52	52	54	56	58	58
PA	167	28	28	30	30	30	32	32	32	34	34	34	36	38	38	40	42	42	44	46	46	48	48	52	52	54	56	58	58
PA	168	28	28	30	30	30	32	32	32	34	34	34	36	38	38	40	42	42	44	46	46	48	48	52	52	54	56	58	58
PA	169	28	28	30	30	30	32	32	32	34	34	34	36	38	38	40	42	42	44	46	46	48	48	52	52	54	56	58	58
PA	170	28	28	30	30	30	32	32	32	34	34	34	36	38	38	40	42	42	44	46	46	48	48	52	52	54	56	58	58
PA	171	28	28	30	30	30	32	32	32	34	34	34	36	38	38	40	42	42	44	46	46	48	48	52	52	54	56	58	58
PA	172	28	28	28	30	30	32	32	32	34	34	34	36	38	38	40	42	42	44	46	46	48	48	52	52	54	56	58	58
PA	173	28	28	28	30	30	32	32	32	34	34	34	36	38	38	40	42	42	44	46	46	48	48	50	52	54	56	58	58
PA	174	28	28	28	30	30	32	32	32	34	34	34	36	38	38	40	42	42	44	44	46	48	48	50	52	54	56	58	58
PA	175	28	28	28	30	30	32	32	32	34	34	34	36	38	38	40	42	42	44	44	46	48	48	50	52	54	56	58	58
PA	176	28	28	28	30	30	32	32	32	34	34	34	36	38	38	40	42	42	44	46	46	48	48	50	52	54	56	58	58
PA	177	26	28	28	30	30	30	32	32	34	34	34	36	38	38	40	42	42	44	44	46	46	48	50	52	54	56	58	58
PA	178	26	28	28	30	30	30	32	32	34	34	34	36	38	38	40	42	42	44	46	46	48	48	50	52	54	56	58	58
PA	179	26	28	28	30	30	30	32	32	34	34	34	36	38	38	40	42	42	44	44	46	46	48	50	52	54	56	58	58
PA	180	26	28	28	30	30	32	32	32	34	34	34	36	38	38	40	42	42	44	44	46	48	48	50	52	54	56	58	58
PA	181	26	28	28	30	30	32	32	32	34	34	36	38	38	40	40	42	44	44	46	46	48	50	52	54	56	58	58	58
PA	182	26	28	28	30	30	32	32	32	34	34	36	38	38	40	40	42	44	44	46	46	48	50	52	54	56	58	58	58
PA	183	26	28	28	30	30	32	32	32	34	34	36	38	38	40	42	42	44	44	46	46	48	50	52	54	56	58	58	58
PA	184	26	28	28	30	30	30	32	32	34	34	36	38	38	40	40	42	44	44	46	46	48	50	52	54	56	58	58	58
PA	185	26	28	28	30	30	30	32	32	32	34	34	36	38	38	40	42	44	44	46	46	48	50	52	54	56	58	58	58
PA	186	26	28	28	30	30	30	32	32	32	34	34	36	38	38	40	42	42	44	44	46	48	50	52	54	56	58	58	58
PA	187	26	28	28	28	30	30	32	32	32	34	34	36	38	38	40	42	42	42	44	46	46	48	50	52	54	56	58	58
PA	188	26	28	28	28	30	30	32	32	32	34	34	36	38	38	40	40	42	44	44	46	46	48	50	52	54	56	58	58
PA	189	26	28	28	28	30	30	32	32	32	34	34	36	38	38	40	40	42	44	44	46	46	48	50	52	54	56	58	58
PA	190	26	28	28	28	30	30	32	32	32	34	34	34	36	38	40	40	42	42	44	46	46	48	50	52	54	56	58	58
PA	191	26	28	28	28	30	30	32	32	32	34	34	36	36	38	40	40	42	42	44	46	46	48	50	52	54	56	58	58
PA	192	26	28	28	28	30	30	32	32	32	34	34	36	38	40	40	42	42	44	46	46	48	50	52	54	56	58	58	58

STATE	Area	1951	1952	1953	1954	1955	1956	1957	1958	1959	1960	1961	1962	1963	1964	1965	1966	1967	1968	1969	1970	1971	1972	1973	1974	1975	1976	1977	78
PA	193	26	28	28	28	30	30	32	32	32	34	34	34	38	40	40	42	42	44	46	46	48	50	52	54	56	58	58	
PA	194	26	28	28	28	30	30	32	32	32	34	34	34	36	38	40	40	42	42	44	46	46	48	50	52	54	56	58	58
PA	195	26	28	28	28	30	30	32	32	32	34	34	34	36	38	40	40	42	42	44	46	46	48	50	52	54	56	58	58
PA	196	26	28	28	28	30	30	32	32	32	34	34	34	38	38	40	40	42	42	44	46	46	48	50	52	54	56	58	58
PA	197	26	28	28	28	30	30	32	32	32	34	34	34	36	38	38	40	40	42	44	46	46	48	50	52	54	56	58	58
PA	198	26	28	28	28	30	30	32	32	32	34	34	34	36	40	38	40	42	42	44	46	46	48	50	52	54	56	58	58
PA	199	26	28	28	28	30	30	32	32	32	34	34	34	36	40	38	40	42	42	44	46	46	48	50	52	54	56	58	58
PA	200	26	28	28	28	30	30	32	32	32	32	34	34	36	40	38	40	42	42	44	44	46	48	50	52	54	56	58	58
PA	201	26	28	28	28	30	30	32	32	32	34	34	34	36	38	40	40	42	42	44	44	46	48	50	52	54	56	56	58
PA	202	26	28	28	28	30	30	30	32	32	34	34	36	38	38	40	40	42	42	44	44	46	48	50	52	54	56	56	58
PA	203	26	28	28	28	30	30	32	32	32	32	34	34	36	38	38	40	42	42	44	44	46	46	48	50	52	54	56	58
PA	204	26	26	28	28	28	30	30	30	32	32	32	34	34	36	38	38	40	42	42	44	44	46	46	50	52	54	54	56
PA	205	26	26	26	28	28	30	30	30	30	32	32	32	34	34	36	38	38	40	42	42	44	46	46	50	52	54	56	58
PA	206	26	26	28	28	28	30	30	30	32	32	32	34	34	36	38	38	40	42	42	44	46	46	50	52	54	54	56	58
PA	207	26	26	28	28	28	30	30	30	32	32	32	34	34	36	38	38	40	42	42	44	46	46	50	52	54	54	56	58
PA	208	26	26	28	28	28	30	30	30	32	32	32	34	34	36	38	38	40	42	42	44	46	46	50	52	54	54	56	56
PA	209	26	26	28	28	28	30	30	30	32	32	32	34	34	36	38	38	40	42	42	44	44	46	46	50	52	54	54	56
PA	210	26	26	28	28	28	28	30	30	32	32	32	34	34	36	38	38	40	42	42	44	44	46	46	50	52	54	54	56
PA	211	26	26	28	28	28	28	30	30	32	32	32	34	34	36	38	38	40	42	42	44	44	46	46	50	52	54	54	56
MD	212	32	34	34	36	36	38	40	40	42	42	44	46	50	52	54	56	58	62	64	66	70	72	76	80	82	86	90	92
MD	213	32	34	34	34	36	38	38	40	40	42	42	44	46	50	52	54	56	60	62	64	68	70	72	76	80	82	86	90
MD	214	32	34	34	34	36	38	38	40	40	42	44	46	50	52	54	56	58	62	64	66	70	72	76	80	82	86	90	02
MD	215	32	32	34	34	36	38	38	40	40	42	44	46	50	50	54	56	58	60	64	66	70	72	76	80	82	86	88	90
MD	216	32	32	34	34	36	36	38	40	40	42	44	46	48	50	54	56	58	60	64	66	70	72	76	78	82	86	88	90
MD	217	32	32	34	34	36	36	38	38	40	42	44	44	48	50	52	56	58	62	64	66	70	72	76	78	82	86	88	90
MD	218	32	32	34	34	36	36	38	40	40	42	42	44	48	50	52	56	58	60	64	66	70	72	76	78	82	86	88	90
MD	219	30	32	32	34	34	36	38	38	40	42	42	44	48	50	52	56	58	60	64	66	68	72	76	78	82	86	88	90
MD	220	30	32	32	34	34	36	38	38	40	40	42	44	48	50	52	56	58	60	62	66	68	72	76	78	82	84	88	90
DE	221	22	22	22	24	24	26	26	26	28	28	30	30	32	32	34	36	38	40	40	42	44	46	52	54	58	60	60	60
DE	222	20	20	22	22	24	24	24	26	26	26	28	28	30	32	34	34	36	38	40	42	44	46	52	54	56	58	60	60
VA	223	42	44	46	48	50	52	54	54	56	56	58	60	62	66	68	70	74	76	80	82	86	88	90	96	02	06	11	15	17
VA	224	40	44	46	48	50	52	52	54	56	56	58	60	62	66	68	70	74	76	80	82	84	88	90	96	02	06	11	15	17
VA	225	40	44	44	46	46	48	52	52	54	54	56	58	58	60	66	68	70	74	76	78	82	84	88	90	96	02	06	11	13	15
VA	226	42	44	44	46	46	48	50	52	54	54	56	56	58	60	66	68	70	74	76	78	82	84	88	90	96	02	06	11	13	15
VA	227	42	44	44	46	46	48	50	52	54	54	56	58	60	64	68	70	74	76	78	82	84	88	90	96	02	06	11	13	15
VA	228	42	44	44	46	46	48	50	52	54	54	56	58	60	64	68	70	74	76	78	82	84	86	90	96	02	06	11	13	15
VA	229	42	42	44	44	46	48	50	52	54	54	56	58	60	64	66	70	72	76	78	82	84	86	90	96	02	04	08	13	15

STATE	Area	1951	1952	1953	1954	1955	1956	1957	1958	1959	1960	1961	1962	1963	1964	1965	1966	1967	1968	1969	1970	1971	1972	1973	1974	1975	1976	1977	78
VA	230	42	42	44	46	48	50	52	52	54	56	58	60	64	66	70	72	76	78	80	84	86	90	96	02	04	08	13	15
VA	231	40	42	44	46	48	50	52	52	54	56	58	60	64	66	70	72	74	78	80	84	86	88	02	98	04	08	13	15
WV & NC	232	54	56	58	58	60	62	64	66	68	70	72	76	78	80	82	84	86	88	92	92	94	02	04	06	11	13	15	
WV	233	54	54	56	58	60	62	64	66	66	68	70	72	76	76	80	82	84	86	88	90	92	94	98	04	06	11	13	15
WV	234	52	54	56	58	60	62	64	64	66	68	70	72	74	76	80	82	84	86	88	90	92	94	98	04	06	11	13	15
WV	235	52	54	56	58	60	62	64	64	66	68	70	70	74	76	78	82	84	86	88	90	92	94	98	02	06	08	13	13
WV	236	52	54	56	58	60	62	62	64	66	66	68	70	74	76	78	80	84	86	88	90	92	94	98	02	06	08	11	13
NC	237	50	52	54	56	58	60	62	66	66	70	72	74	76	80	82	86	90	92	94	98	02	04	11	15	19	23	27	29
NC	238	50	52	54	56	58	60	62	64	66	68	70	74	78	80	82	86	90	92	94	98	02	04	11	15	19	23	27	29
NC	239	48	52	54	54	58	60	62	64	66	68	70	72	76	80	82	86	90	92	94	98	02	04	11	15	19	23	27	29
NC	240	50	50	54	54	58	60	62	64	66	68	70	72	78	80	82	86	88	92	94	98	02	04	11	15	19	23	25	29
NC	241	48	50	52	54	58	60	62	64	66	68	70	72	76	80	82	86	88	92	94	98	02	04	11	15	19	23	25	27
NC	242	50	50	52	54	58	60	62	64	66	68	70	72	76	78	82	86	88	92	94	98	02	04	11	15	19	23	25	27
NC	243	48	50	52	54	56	60	62	64	66	68	70	72	76	78	82	86	88	90	94	96	02	04	11	15	19	23	25	27
NC	244	48	50	52	54	56	60	62	64	66	68	70	72	76	78	82	86	88	90	94	96	02	04	11	15	17	21	25	27
NC	245	48	50	52	54	56	60	62	64	66	68	70	72	76	78	82	84	88	90	94	96	02	04	11	15	17	21	25	27
NC	246	48	50	52	54	56	58	62	64	66	68	70	72	76	78	82	84	88	90	92	96	02	04	11	15	17	21	25	27
SC	247	54	52	58	58	62	64	66	68	70	74	76	78	82	84	88	94	96	98	04	06	11	13	19	25	31	33	37	39
SC	248	54	54	56	58	62	64	66	68	70	72	76	78	82	84	88	94	96	98	04	06	11	13	19	25	29	33	37	39
SC	249	52	52	56	58	62	64	66	68	70	72	74	78	82	84	88	92	96	98	02	06	08	13	19	25	29	33	37	39
SC	250	52	52	56	58	60	64	66	68	70	72	74	78	82	84	88	92	94	98	02	06	08	13	19	25	29	33	35	39
SC	251	52	54	56	58	60	64	66	68	70	72	74	76	82	84	88	94	94	96	02	06	08	13	19	25	29	33	35	39
GA	252	52	54	56	56	58	60	64	64	66	68	70	72	76	78	82	88	88	92	94	98	02	06	15	19	23	27	29	31
GA	253	52	54	54	56	58	60	62	64	66	68	70	72	76	78	82	88	88	92	94	96	02	06	15	19	23	27	29	31
GA	254	50	52	54	56	58	60	62	64	66	68	70	72	76	78	82	88	88	92	94	98	02	04	15	19	23	27	29	31
GA	255	52	52	54	56	58	60	62	64	66	68	70	72	76	78	82	88	88	92	94	96	02	04	15	19	23	27	29	31
GA	256	52	52	54	56	58	60	62	64	66	68	68	70	74	78	80	88	88	90	94	96	02	04	15	19	23	27	29	31
GA	257	52	52	54	56	58	60	62	64	64	66	68	70	74	76	80	88	88	90	94	96	02	04	15	19	23	27	29	31
GA	258	50	52	54	56	58	60	62	64	64	66	68	70	74	76	80	88	88	90	94	96	02	04	17	21	23	27	29	31
GA	259	50	52	54	56	58	60	62	62	64	66	68	70	74	76	80	86	86	90	92	96	02	04	17	21	25	27	27	29
GA	260	50	52	54	54	56	60	62	62	64	66	68	70	74	76	80	86	86	90	92	96	02	04	17	21	25	25	27	29
FL	261	48	50	52	54	58	60	62	64	68	70	74	78	88	94	98	13	13	19	23	31	35	39	51	61	67	75	81	87
FL	262	50	50	52	54	58	60	62	64	66	70	72	80	866	94	98	13	13	19	23	29	35	39	51	59	67	75	81	87
FL	263	48	50	52	54	56	60	62	64	66	70	72	78	88	92	98	13	13	17	23	29	35	39	51	59	67	75	81	85

STATE	Area	1951	1952	1953	1954	1955	1956	1957	1958	1959	1960	1961	1962	1963	1964	1965	1966	1967	1968	1969	1970	1971	1972	1973	1974	1975	1976	1977	78
FL	264	48	50	52	54	56	60	62	64	66	70	72	78	86	90	98	13	13	17	23	29	35	39	51	59	67	75	81	85
FL	265	48	50	52	54	56	60	62	64	66	68	72	76	86	92	98	13	13	17	23	29	35	39	51	59	67	73	81	85
FL	266	48	50	52	52	56	58	60	64	66	70	72	76	86	92	98	13	13	17	23	29	35	39	51	59	67	73	81	85
FL	267	48	50	50	54	56	58	60	62	66	68	72	76	86	92	98	11	11	17	23	29	33	39	49	59	67	73	79	85
OH	268	30	32	32	34	34	36	36	38	38	40	40	42	44	46	50	52	52	54	56	58	58	60	64	66	68	72	72	74
OH	269	30	32	32	34	34	36	36	38	38	40	40	42	44	46	50	52	52	54	54	56	58	60	64	66	68	72	72	74
OH	270	30	32	32	34	34	36	36	38	38	40	40	40	44	46	50	52	52	54	54	56	58	60	64	66	68	72	72	74
OH	271	30	32	32	34	34	36	36	38	38	38	40	40	44	46	50	52	52	54	54	56	58	60	64	66	68	72	72	74
OH	272	30	32	32	34	34	36	36	38	38	38	40	40	44	46	50	52	52	54	56	56	58	60	64	66	68	72	72	74
OH	273	30	32	32	34	34	36	36	36	38	38	40	40	44	46	50	52	52	54	54	56	58	60	64	66	68	72	72	74
OH	274	30	32	32	34	34	36	36	38	38	38	40	40	44	46	50	52	52	54	54	56	58	60	64	66	68	70	72	74
OH	275	30	32	32	34	34	36	36	36	38	38	40	40	44	46	50	52	52	52	54	56	58	60	64	66	68	70	72	74
OH	276	30	32	32	34	36	36	36	36	38	38	40	40	44	46	48	50	52	52	54	56	58	60	64	66	68	70	72	74
OH	277	30	32	32	32	36	36	36	36	38	38	40	40	44	46	48	50	52	52	54	56	58	60	64	66	68	70	72	74
OH	278	30	32	32	32	36	36	36	36	38	38	40	40	44	46	48	50	50	52	54	56	58	60	64	66	68	70	72	72
OH	279	30	32	32	32	34	34	36	36	38	38	40	40	44	46	48	50	50	52	56	56	58	60	64	66	68	70	72	72
OH	280	30	32	32	32	36	36	36	36	38	38	40	40	44	46	48	50	50	52	54	56	58	60	64	66	68	70	72	72
OH	281	30	32	32	32	36	36	36	36	38	38	40	40	44	46	48	50	50	52	54	56	58	60	64	66	68	70	72	72
OH	282	30	32	32	32	34	34	36	36	38	38	40	40	48	46	46	50	50	52	54	56	58	60	64	66	68	70	72	72
OH	283	30	30	32	32	34	34	36	36	38	38	40	40	48	46	48	50	50	52	54	56	58	60	64	66	68	70	72	72
OH	284	30	30	32	32	34	34	36	36	38	38	40	40	48	46	48	50	50	52	54	56	58	58	64	66	68	70	72	72
OH	285	30	30	32	32	34	34	36	36	38	38	38	40	48	46	48	50	50	52	54	56	58	58	64	66	68	70	72	72
OH	286	30	30	32	32	34	34	36	36	38	38	40	40	48	46	46	50	50	52	54	56	58	58	64	66	68	70	72	72
OH	287	30	30	32	32	34	34	36	36	38	38	38	40	48	46	46	48	50	52	54	56	58	58	64	66	68	70	72	72
OH	288	30	30	32	32	34	34	36	36	38	38	38	40	48	46	46	48	50	52	54	56	58	58	64	66	68	70	72	72
OH	289	30	30	32	32	34	34	36	36	38	38	38	40	48	44	46	48	50	52	54	56	58	58	64	66	68	70	72	72
OH	290	30	30	32	32	34	34	36	36	38	38	38	40	48	44	48	48	50	52	54	56	58	58	64	66	68	70	72	72
OH	291	30	30	32	32	34	34	36	36	36	38	38	40	48	44	48	48	50	52	54	56	56	58	64	66	68	70	72	72
OH	292	30	30	32	32	34	34	36	36	36	38	38	40	48	44	48	48	50	52	54	56	58	58	62	66	68	70	72	72
OH	293	30	30	32	32	34	34	36	36	36	38	38	40	42	44	48	48	50	52	54	56	56	58	62	66	68	70	72	72
OH	294	30	30	32	32	34	34	36	36	36	38	38	40	44	44	48	48	50	52	54	56	58	58	62	64	68	70	72	72
OH	295	28	30	32	32	32	34	36	36	36	38	38	40	42	44	48	48	50	52	54	56	56	58	62	64	68	70	70	72
OH	296	28	30	32	32	34	34	34	36	36	38	38	40	44	44	48	48	50	52	54	56	56	58	62	64	68	70	70	72
OH	297	28	30	32	32	32	34	34	36	36	38	38	40	44	44	48	48	50	52	54	54	56	58	62	64	68	70	70	72
OH	298	28	30	32	32	32	34	34	36	36	38	38	40	44	44	48	48	50	52	54	54	56	58	62	64	66	70	70	72
OH	299	28	30	32	32	32	34	34	36	36	38	38	40	42	44	48	48	50	52	54	54	56	58	62	64	66	70	70	72
OH	300	30	30	32	32	34	34	36	36	38	38	40	44	44	48	48	50	52	54	54	56	58	58	62	64	66	70	70	72
OH	301	28	30	30	32	32	34	34	36	36	38	38	40	44	44	46	48	50	52	54	56	56	58	62	64	66	70	70	72
OH	302	28	30	30	32	32	34	34	36	36	38	38	40	44	44	46	48	50	52	54	54	56	58	62	64	66	70	70	72

STATE	Area	1951	1952	1953	1954	1955	1956	1957	1958	1959	1960	1961	1962	1963	1964	1965	1966	1967	1968	1969	1970	1971	1972	1973	1974	1975	1976	1977	78
IN	303	36	36	38	38	40	42	42	44	44	46	48	52	52	54	48	58	60	62	64	66	58	72	74	76	80	82	82
IN	304	34	36	38	38	40	42	42	44	44	46	46	48	52	52	54	56	58	60	62	64	66	68	72	74	76	80	82	82
IN	305	34	36	38	38	40	42	42	44	44	46	46	48	52	52	54	56	58	60	62	64	66	68	72	74	76	80	80	82
IN	306	34	36	36	38	40	40	42	42	44	46	46	48	50	52	54	56	58	60	62	64	66	68	72	74	76	80	80	82
IN	307	34	36	36	38	40	40	42	42	44	46	46	48	50	52	54	56	58	60	62	64	66	68	72	74	76	78	80	82
IN	308	34	36	36	38	40	40	42	42	44	46	46	48	50	52	54	56	58	60	62	64	66	68	72	74	76	78	80	82
IN	309	34	36	36	38	38	40	42	42	44	46	46	48	50	52	54	56	58	60	62	64	66	68	72	74	76	78	80	82
IN	310	34	36	36	38	38	40	42	42	44	44	46	48	50	52	54	56	58	60	62	64	66	68	72	74	76	78	80	82
IN	311	34	36	36	36	38	40	42	42	44	44	46	46	50	52	54	56	58	60	62	64	66	68	72	74	76	78	80	82
IN	312	34	34	36	38	38	40	42	42	44	44	46	46	50	52	54	56	58	58	62	64	66	68	70	74	76	78	80	82
IN	313	34	34	36	36	38	40	42	42	44	44	46	46	50	52	54	56	58	58	60	64	66	68	70	74	76	78	80	82
IN	314	34	34	36	36	38	40	40	42	42	44	46	46	50	52	54	56	58	60	62	66	66	68	70	72	76	78	80	82
IN	315	34	34	36	36	38	40	40	42	42	44	46	46	50	52	54	54	56	58	60	62	66	68	70	72	74	78	80	82
IN	316	34	34	36	36	38	40	40	42	42	44	44	46	50	50	52	54	56	58	60	62	64	66	70	72	74	78	80	80
IN	317	34	34	36	36	38	40	40	42	42	44	46	48	50	52	54	56	58	60	62	66	66	70	72	74	78	80	80	
IL	318	28	30	30	32	32	34	34	34	36	36	38	38	40	42	44	46	46	48	50	52	54	54	58	60	62	64	66	66
IL	319	28	30	30	32	32	34	34	34	36	36	38	38	40	42	44	46	46	48	50	52	52	54	58	60	62	64	66	66
IL	320	28	30	30	30	32	34	34	34	36	36	38	38	40	42	44	46	46	48	50	52	52	54	58	60	62	66	66	66
IL	321	28	30	30	30	32	34	34	34	36	36	38	38	40	42	44	46	46	48	50	52	54	54	58	60	62	64	66	66
IL	322	28	30	30	30	32	32	34	34	36	36	38	38	40	42	44	46	46	48	50	52	54	54	58	60	62	64	66	66
IL	323	28	30	30	30	32	34	34	34	36	36	36	38	40	42	44	46	46	48	50	52	54	54	58	60	62	64	64	66
IL	324	28	30	30	30	32	34	34	34	36	36	36	38	40	42	44	46	46	48	50	52	52	54	58	60	62	64	64	66
IL	325	28	30	30	30	32	34	34	34	36	36	36	38	40	42	44	46	46	48	50	52	52	54	58	00	02	04	04	00
IL	326	28	30	30	30	32	32	34	34	36	36	36	38	40	42	44	46	46	48	50	52	54	54	58	60	62	64	64	66
IL	327	28	30	30	30	32	32	34	34	36	36	36	38	40	42	44	46	46	48	50	52	54	54	58	60	62	64	64	66
IL	328	28	30	30	30	32	32	34	34	36	36	36	38	40	42	42	44	46	48	50	52	52	54	58	58	60	64	64	66
IL	329	28	28	30	30	32	32	34	34	36	36	36	38	40	42	42	44	46	48	50	52	52	54	58	58	60	64	64	66
IL	330	28	28	30	30	32	32	34	34	34	36	36	38	40	42	44	44	46	48	50	50	52	54	58	58	60	64	64	66
IL	331	28	28	30	30	32	32	34	34	36	36	36	38	40	42	44	44	46	48	50	52	52	54	58	58	60	64	64	66
IL	332	28	28	30	30	32	32	34	34	34	36	36	38	40	42	42	44	46	48	50	52	52	54	58	58	60	64	64	66
IL	333	28	28	30	30	32	32	34	34	36	36	36	38	40	42	42	44	46	48	50	50	52	54	56	58	60	62	64	66
IL	334	28	28	30	30	32	32	34	34	34	36	36	38	40	42	42	44	46	48	50	50	52	54	56	58	60	62	64	66
IL	335	28	28	30	30	32	32	34	34	34	36	36	38	40	42	42	44	46	48	50	50	52	54	56	58	60	62	64	66
IL	336	28	28	30	30	32	32	34	34	34	36	36	38	40	42	42	44	46	48	50	50	52	54	56	58	60	62	64	66
IL	337	28	28	30	30	32	32	34	34	34	36	36	38	40	42	42	44	46	48	48	50	52	54	56	58	60	62	64	66
IL	338	28	28	30	30	32	32	34	34	34	36	36	38	40	42	42	44	46	48	50	50	52	54	56	58	60	62	64	66
IL	339	28	28	30	30	32	32	34	34	34	36	36	38	40	40	42	44	46	46	50	50	52	54	56	58	60	62	64	66
IL	340	28	28	30	30	32	32	34	34	34	36	36	38	40	40	42	44	46	46	48	50	52	54	56	58	60	62	64	66

STATE	Area	1951	1952	1953	1954	1955	1956	1957	1958	1959	1960	1961	1962	1963	1964	1965	1966	1967	1968	1969	1970	1971	1972	1973	1974	1975	1976	1977	78
IL	341	28	28	30	30	32	32	32	34	34	36	36	38	40	40	42	44	46	46	48	50	52	54	56	58	60	62	64	66
IL	342	28	28	30	30	32	32	32	34	34	36	36	38	40	40	42	44	46	46	48	50	52	54	56	58	60	62	64	66
IL	343	28	28	30	30	32	32	32	34	34	36	36	38	40	40	42	44	46	46	48	50	52	54	56	58	60	62	64	66
IL	344	28	28	30	30	30	32	32	34	34	36	36	38	40	40	42	44	46	48	48	50	52	54	56	58	60	62	64	66
IL	345	28	28	30	30	30	32	32	34	34	36	36	38	40	40	42	44	46	46	48	50	52	54	56	58	60	62	64	66
IL	346	28	28	30	30	30	32	32	34	34	36	36	36	40	40	42	44	46	46	48	50	52	54	56	58	60	62	64	66
IL	347	28	28	30	30	30	32	32	34	34	36	36	36	40	40	42	44	46	46	48	50	52	54	56	58	60	62	64	66
IL	348	28	28	30	30	30	32	32	34	34	36	36	36	40	40	42	44	46	46	48	50	52	54	56	58	60	62	64	66
IL	349	28	28	28	30	30	32	32	34	34	36	36	36	40	40	42	44	46	46	48	50	52	54	56	58	60	62	64	66
IL	350	26	28	28	30	30	32	32	34	34	34	36	36	40	40	42	44	46	46	48	50	52	52	56	58	60	62	64	66
IL	351	26	28	28	30	30	32	32	34	34	34	36	36	40	40	42	44	46	46	48	50	52	52	56	58	60	62	64	64
IL	352	28	28	28	30	30	32	32	34	34	34	36	36	38	40	42	44	46	46	48	50	52	52	56	58	60	62	64	64
IL	353	28	28	28	30	30	32	32	34	34	34	36	36	40	40	42	44	44	46	48	50	52	52	56	58	60	62	64	64
IL	354	26	28	28	30	30	32	32	34	34	34	36	36	40	40	42	44	44	46	48	50	52	52	56	58	60	62	64	64
IL	355	28	28	28	30	30	32	32	32	34	34	36	36	40	40	42	44	44	46	48	50	52	52	56	58	60	62	64	64
IL	356	26	28	28	30	30	32	32	32	34	34	36	36	40	40	42	44	44	46	48	50	52	52	56	58	60	62	64	64
IL	357	26	28	28	30	30	32	32	34	34	34	36	36	40	40	42	44	44	46	48	50	52	52	56	58	60	62	64	64
IL	358	26	28	28	30	30	32	32	32	34	34	36	36	38	40	42	44	44	46	48	50	52	52	56	58	60	62	64	64
IL	359	26	28	28	30	30	32	32	32	34	34	36	36	40	40	42	44	46	46	48	50	52	52	56	58	60	62	64	64
IL	360	26	28	28	30	30	32	32	32	34	34	36	36	38	40	42	44	44	46	48	50	52	52	56	58	60	62	64	64
IL	361	26	28	28	30	30	32	32	32	34	34	36	36	38	40	42	44	46	46	48	50	52	52	56	58	60	62	64	64
MI	362	34	36	36	38	38	40	42	42	44	44	44	46	48	50	54	56	56	60	62	62	64	66	72	74	76	80	82	84
MI	363	34	36	36	38	38	40	42	42	42	44	44	46	48	50	52	54	58	58	60	64	64	66	72	74	76	80	82	84
MI	364	34	36	36	38	38	40	42	42	42	44	44	46	48	50	52	54	56	60	60	62	64	66	72	74	76	80	82	84
MI	365	34	34	36	36	38	40	40	42	42	44	44	46	50	50	52	54	56	60	60	62	64	66	72	74	76	80	82	84
MI	366	34	34	36	36	38	40	40	42	42	44	44	46	48	50	52	54	56	58	60	62	64	66	70	74	76	80	82	84
MI	367	34	34	36	36	38	40	40	42	42	44	44	46	48	50	52	54	56	58	60	62	64	66	70	74	76	80	82	84
MI	368	34	34	36	36	38	40	40	42	42	44	44	46	48	50	52	54	56	58	60	62	64	66	70	74	76	80	82	84
MI	369	34	34	36	36	38	40	40	42	42	44	44	46	48	50	52	54	56	58	60	62	64	66	70	74	76	80	82	84
MI	370	34	34	36	36	38	40	40	42	42	44	44	46	48	50	52	54	56	58	60	62	64	66	70	74	76	78	82	84
MI	371	34	34	36	36	38	40	40	42	42	44	44	46	48	50	52	54	56	58	60	62	64	66	70	72	76	78	82	84
MI	372	32	34	36	36	38	40	40	42	42	44	44	46	48	50	52	54	56	58	60	62	64	66	70	72	76	78	82	84
MI	373	32	34	36	36	38	40	40	42	42	44	44	46	48	50	52	54	56	58	60	62	64	66	70	72	74	78	82	82
MI	374	34	34	36	36	38	40	40	42	42	44	44	46	48	50	52	54	56	58	60	62	64	66	70	72	74	78	82	82
MI	375	34	34	36	36	38	40	40	40	42	44	44	46	48	50	52	54	56	58	60	62	64	66	70	72	74	78	82	82
MI	376	32	34	36	36	38	40	40	40	42	44	44	46	48	50	52	54	56	58	60	62	64	66	70	72	74	78	82	82
MI	377	32	34	36	36	38	38	40	40	42	42	44	46	48	50	52	54	56	58	60	62	64	66	70	72	74	78	80	82
MI	378	32	34	36	36	38	38	40	40	42	42	44	46	48	50	52	54	56	58	60	62	64	64	70	72	74	78	80	82
MI	379	32	34	36	36	38	38	40	40	42	42	44	44	48	50	52	54	56	58	60	62	64	64	70	72	74	78	80	82

STATE	Area	1951	1952	1953	1954	1955	1956	1957	1958	1959	1960	1961	1962	1963	1964	1965	1966	1967	1968	1969	1970	1971	1972	1973	1974	1975	1976	1977	78
MI	380	32	34	34	36	38	38	40	40	42	42	44	44	48	50	52	54	56	58	60	62	64	64	70	72	74	78	80	80
MI	381	32	34	34	36	38	38	40	40	42	42	44	44	48	50	52	54	56	58	60	62	64	64	70	72	74	78	80	80
MI	382	32	34	34	36	38	38	40	40	42	42	44	44	48	50	52	54	56	58	60	62	64	64	70	72	74	78	80	80
MI	383	32	34	34	36	38	38	40	40	42	42	44	44	48	50	52	54	56	58	60	62	64	64	70	72	74	78	80	80
MI	384	32	34	34	36	36	38	40	40	42	42	44	44	48	50	52	54	56	58	60	60	64	64	70	72	74	78	80	80
MI	385	32	34	34	36	36	38	40	40	42	42	44	44	48	50	50	54	54	58	60	60	62	64	70	72	74	78	80	80
MI	386	32	34	34	36	36	38	40	40	40	42	44	44	48	48	52	54	54	58	60	60	64	64	70	72	74	78	80	80
WI	387	32	34	34	36	36	38	40	40	42	42	44	44	48	50	52	54	56	58	60	62	64	66	70	74	76	80	82	80
WI	388	32	32	34	34	36	38	40	40	42	42	44	44	48	50	52	54	56	58	60	62	64	66	70	74	76	80	82	80
WI	389	32	32	34	34	36	38	40	40	42	42	44	44	48	50	52	54	56	58	60	62	64	66	70	74	76	80	82	80
WI	390	32	32	34	34	36	38	40	40	40	42	44	44	48	50	52	54	56	58	60	62	64	66	70	74	76	80	80	80
WI	391	32	32	34	34	36	38	38	40	40	42	44	44	48	50	52	54	56	58	60	62	64	66	70	74	76	78	80	80
WI	392	32	32	34	34	36	38	38	40	40	42	44	44	48	50	52	54	56	58	60	62	64	66	70	72	76	78	80	80
WI	393	32	32	34	34	36	38	38	40	40	42	44	44	48	50	52	54	56	58	60	62	64	66	70	72	76	78	80	80
WI	394	32	32	32	34	36	38	38	40	40	42	44	44	48	50	52	54	56	58	60	62	64	66	70	72	76	78	80	80
WI	395	30	32	32	34	36	36	38	40	40	42	44	44	48	50	52	54	56	58	60	62	64	64	70	72	76	78	80	80
WI	396	30	32	32	34	36	38	38	38	40	42	44	44	48	50	50	54	56	58	58	60	64	64	70	72	74	78	80	80
WI	397	30	32	32	34	36	36	38	38	40	42	44	44	46	48	50	54	56	56	58	60	62	64	70	72	74	78	80	80
WI	398	30	32	32	34	34	36	38	38	40	40	44	44	48	48	50	52	54	58	60	60	62	64	70	72	74	78	80	80
WI	399	30	32	32	34	34	36	38	38	40	40	44	44	48	48	50	54	54	56	58	60	64	64	70	72	74	78	80	80
KY	400	44	46	48	50	52	54	56	56	58	60	60	62	66	68	72	74	76	78	82	84	86	88	94	98	04	06	08	11
KY	401	44	46	48	48	52	54	56	56	58	58	60	62	66	68	70	74	76	78	80	84	86	88	94	98	04	06	08	11
KY	402	44	46	48	48	50	54	54	56	58	58	60	62	66	68	70	74	76	78	80	84	86	88	94	98	04	06	00	11
KY	403	42	46	46	48	50	54	54	56	56	58	60	62	66	66	70	72	76	78	80	82	86	88	92	96	04	06	08	11
KY	404	44	44	46	48	50	52	54	56	56	58	60	62	64	66	70	72	74	78	80	82	86	88	92	96	02	06	08	11
KY	405	44	44	46	48	50	52	54	54	56	58	60	62	64	66	70	72	76	78	80	82	86	88	92	96	02	06	08	11
KY	406	42	44	46	48	50	52	54	56	56	58	60	62	64	66	70	72	74	76	80	82	84	88	92	96	02	06	08	11
KY	407	42	44	46	48	50	52	54	54	56	58	58	60	64	66	68	72	74	76	78	82	84	86	92	96	02	04	08	08
TN	408	54	56	58	58	62	64	66	66	68	70	72	74	78	80	84	86	90	92	96	98	02	06	15	19	23	27	08	29
TN	409	54	54	54	58	60	64	66	66	68	70	72	74	78	80	84	88	90	92	94	98	04	06	15	19	23	27	29	29
TN	410	54	54	54	58	62	64	66	66	68	70	72	74	78	80	84	88	90	92	94	98	02	04	13	19	23	25	27	29
TN	411	52	54	54	58	60	62	64	66	68	70	72	74	78	80	84	88	90	92	94	98	02	04	13	19	21	25	27	29
TN	412	52	54	54	58	60	62	64	66	68	70	72	74	78	80	84	86	88	92	94	98	02	04	13	17	21	25	27	29
TN	413	52	54	54	58	60	62	64	66	68	70	70	74	76	80	82	86	88	92	94	96	02	04	13	17	21	25	27	29
TN	414	52	54	54	58	60	62	64	66	68	70	72	72	76	80	84	86	88	92	94	96	02	04	13	17	21	25	27	29
TN	415	52	54	54	58	60	62	64	66	68	68	70	72	76	78	82	86	88	90	94	96	02	04	13	17	21	25	27	29

GEOGRAPHIC AND CHRONOLOGICAL DISTRIBUTION OF SSNs

STATE	Area	1951	1952	1953	1954	1955	1956	1957	1958	1959	1960	1961	1962	1963	1964	1965	1966	1967	1968	1969	1970	1971	1972	1973	1974	1975	1976	1977	78
AL	416	44	46	46	48	50	52	54	54	56	58	60	62	64	66	70	72	74	76	78	80	82	84	90	94	96	02	04	06
AL	417	44	44	44	48	50	52	54	54	56	58	60	60	64	66	70	72	74	76	78	80	82	84	90	94	96	02	04	04
AL	418	42	44	44	48	50	52	54	54	56	58	60	60	64	66	68	72	74	76	78	80	82	84	90	94	96	98	02	04
AL	419	44	44	44	48	50	52	52	54	56	58	58	60	64	66	70	72	74	74	78	80	82	84	90	94	96	98	02	04
AL	420	44	44	44	48	50	52	52	54	56	58	58	60	64	66	68	70	72	76	76	80	82	84	90	92	96	98	02	04
AL	421	42	44	44	48	50	50	52	54	56	58	58	60	64	64	68	70	74	74	76	78	80	82	90	92	96	98	02	04
AL	422	42	44	44	46	48	50	52	54	56	56	58	60	62	64	68	72	74	74	76	78	80	82	90	92	96	98	02	04
AL	423	42	44	44	46	48	50	52	54	54	56	58	60	62	64	68	70	72	74	76	78	80	84	88	92	94	98	02	04
AL	424	42	44	44	46	48	50	52	54	54	56	58	60	62	64	68	70	72	74	76	78	80	82	88	92	94	98	02	04
MS	425	62	64	64	70	74	78	82	84	86	88	90	94	98	98	98	98	98	98	98	02	08	11	17	21	25	29	31	33
MS	426	60	64	68	70	74	78	80	82	86	88	90	92	98	98	98	98	98	98	98	02	06	11	17	21	25	29	31	33
MS	427	60	64	66	68	74	78	80	82	84	88	90	92	96	98	98	98	98	98	98	02	06	11	15	21	25	29	29	31
MS	428	62	64	66	68	74	76	80	82	84	86	90	92	96	98	98	98	98	98	98	02	06	11	15	19	23	29	29	31
AR	429	62	62	66	66	70	74	74	76	78	80	82	86	88	90	96	98	02	04	08	11	15	17	25	29	33	35	39	41
AR	430	60	62	64	66	70	72	74	76	78	80	82	84	88	90	96	98	02	04	06	11	13	17	23	27	31	35	37	39
AR	431	60	62	64	66	70	72	74	76	78	80	82	84	88	90	94	98	02	04	06	11	13	17	23	27	31	35	37	39
AR	432	60	62	64	66	68	72	74	76	76	78	82	84	88	90	94	98	02	04	06	11	13	15	23	27	31	35	37	39
LA	433	48	50	52	54	56	58	60	60	62	64	66	68	72	74	80	84	86	90	94	98	02	06	15	19	25	29	33	35
LA	434	48	50	52	52	54	56	58	60	62	64	64	68	72	74	78	82	86	90	92	98	02	06	15	19	25	29	33	35
LA	435	48	50	52	52	54	56	58	60	62	64	66	66	72	74	78	82	86	88	92	96	02	06	13	19	25	29	31	35
LA	436	48	50	52	52	54	56	58	60	62	62	64	66	72	74	76	82	86	88	92	96	02	06	13	19	23	29	31	35
LA	437	48	48	50	52	54	56	58	60	60	62	64	66	72	74	78	82	84	88	92	96	02	06	13	19	23	29	31	35
LA	438	48	48	50	52	54	56	58	60	60	62	64	68	70	74	78	82	86	88	92	96	02	06	13	19	23	27	31	33
LA	439	48	48	48	50	52	54	56	58	60	62	64	66	70	74	78	82	84	88	92	96	02	04	13	17	23	27	31	33
OK	440	34	36	36	38	38	40	42	42	44	44	46	46	48	50	52	54	54	56	58	60	62	62	66	68	70	72	74	74
OK	441	34	34	36	36	38	40	40	42	42	44	44	46	48	50	52	54	54	56	58	60	62	62	66	68	70	72	74	74
OK	442	32	34	36	36	38	40	40	42	42	44	44	46	48	50	52	54	54	56	58	60	60	62	66	68	70	72	74	74
OK	443	34	34	36	36	38	40	40	42	42	44	44	46	48	48	50	52	54	56	58	58	60	62	66	68	70	72	74	74
OK	444	32	34	36	36	38	40	40	42	42	42	44	46	48	48	50	52	54	56	56	58	60	62	66	68	70	72	72	74
OK	445	34	34	36	36	38	38	40	40	42	42	44	46	46	48	50	52	54	56	56	58	60	62	66	68	70	72	72	74
OK	446	34	34	34	36	38	38	40	40	42	42	44	44	46	48	50	52	54	54	56	58	60	62	64	68	70	72	72	74
OK	447	32	34	34	36	38	38	40	40	42	42	44	44	46	48	50	52	54	54	56	58	60	62	64	66	70	72	72	74
OK	448	32	34	34	36	36	38	40	40	42	42	44	44	46	48	50	52	52	54	56	58	58	60	64	66	70	70	72	74
TX	449	54	56	58	58	62	64	66	68	70	72	74	76	80	84	88	92	96	98	06	08	13	15	25	29	35	39	41	45
TX	450	52	56	58	58	62	64	66	68	70	72	74	76	80	84	88	92	94	98	04	06	13	15	23	29	35	39	41	45

STATE	Area	1951	1952	1953	1954	1955	1956	1957	1958	1959	1960	1961	1962	1963	1964	1965	1966	1967	1968	1969	1970	1971	1972	1973	1974	1975	1976	1977	78
TX	451	54	56	58	58	62	64	66	68	70	72	74	76	82	84	88	92	96	98	04	08	13	15	23	29	33	39	41	45
TX	452	52	56	58	58	62	64	66	68	70	72	74	76	80	84	88	92	96	98	04	08	11	15	23	29	33	39	41	45
TX	453	54	54	56	58	62	64	66	68	70	72	74	76	80	84	88	92	94	98	04	08	13	15	23	29	33	39	41	43
TX	454	52	56	56	58	62	64	66	68	70	72	72	76	80	82	88	92	94	98	04	06	13	15	23	29	33	39	41	43
TX	455	54	54	54	58	60	64	66	68	68	72	72	76	80	84	88	92	94	98	04	08	13	15	23	29	33	37	41	43
TX	456	54	54	56	58	60	64	66	68	68	70	74	76	80	84	88	92	94	98	04	06	13	15	23	29	33	37	41	43
TX	457	52	54	56	58	60	64	66	68	68	70	72	76	80	82	88	90	94	98	04	06	13	15	23	29	33	37	41	43
TX	458	52	54	58	58	60	64	66	66	68	70	72	76	80	82	88	92	94	98	04	06	13	15	23	29	33	37	41	43
TX	459	52	54	56	58	60	64	66	66	68	70	72	76	80	82	86	92	94	96	04	06	11	15	23	29	33	37	41	43
TX	460	52	54	56	58	60	64	66	66	68	70	72	74	80	82	86	92	94	98	04	06	11	15	23	29	33	37	41	43
TX	461	52	54	56	58	60	62	66	66	68	70	72	74	80	82	86	90	94	98	02	06	11	13	23	29	33	37	39	43
TX	462	52	54	56	58	60	62	64	66	68	70	72	74	80	82	86	90	94	98	02	06	11	13	23	29	33	37	39	43
TX	463	52	54	56	58	60	62	64	66	68	70	72	74	80	82	88	90	94	98	02	06	11	13	23	29	33	37	39	43
TX	464	52	54	56	58	60	64	64	66	68	70	72	76	80	82	86	90	94	96	02	06	11	13	23	27	33	37	39	43
TX	465	52	54	56	58	60	62	64	66	68	70	72	74	80	82	86	90	92	96	02	06	11	13	23	27	33	37	39	43
TX	466	52	54	56	58	60	62	64	66	68	70	72	74	80	82	86	90	94	98	02	06	08	13	23	27	33	37	39	43
TX	467	52	54	56	56	60	44	64	66	68	70	72	74	78	82	84	90	94	96	02	06	11	13	23	27	33	37	39	43
MN	468	36	38	38	40	42	44	46	46	48	48	50	52	56	56	58	62	64	66	68	70	72	74	80	82	84	84	90	90
MN	469	36	36	38	40	42	44	46	46	48	48	50	52	56	56	58	62	64	66	68	70	72	74	78	82	84	84	90	90
MN	470	34	36	38	40	42	44	44	46	48	48	50	52	54	56	58	62	64	64	68	70	72	74	78	82	84	84	88	90
MN	471	36	36	38	38	42	44	44	46	46	48	50	50	54	56	58	60	62	64	66	70	70	72	78	82	84	84	88	90
MN	472	34	36	38	38	42	44	44	46	46	48	50	52	54	56	58	60	62	64	66	68	70	72	78	82	84	84	88	90
MN	473	34	34	36	38	38	40	44	44	46	48	50	50	54	56	58	60	62	64	66	68	70	72	78	80	84	84	88	90
MN	474	36	36	38	38	40	42	44	44	46	48	48	50	54	56	58	60	62	64	66	68	70	72	78	80	84	84	88	90
MN	475	34	36	36	38	40	42	44	44	46	48	48	50	54	56	58	60	62	64	66	68	70	72	78	80	84	84	88	90
MN	476	34	36	36	38	40	42	44	44	46	48	48	50	54	56	58	60	62	64	66	68	70	72	78	80	84	84	88	90
MN	477	34	36	36	38	40	42	44	44	46	46	48	50	52	56	56	60	62	64	66	68	70	72	78	80	82	82	88	90
IA	478	36	38	40	42	46	48	50	50	52	52	54	56	62	62	66	68	70	72	74	76	78	78	84	86	88	88	94	94
IA	479	36	38	40	42	44	48	48	50	52	52	54	56	58	62	66	68	70	72	74	74	78	78	84	86	88	88	94	94
IA	480	38	38	40	40	44	48	48	50	50	52	54	56	60	62	64	66	68	70	72	74	76	78	84	86	88	88	94	94
IA	481	38	38	40	40	44	48	48	50	50	52	54	54	58	62	64	66	68	72	72	74	76	78	82	86	88	88	92	94
IA	482	38	38	40	40	44	48	48	50	50	52	54	54	58	62	64	66	68	70	72	74	76	78	82	86	88	88	92	94
IA	483	36	38	40	40	44	48	48	48	50	52	52	54	58	62	64	66	68	70	72	74	76	78	82	86	88	88	92	94
IA	484	36	38	38	40	44	46	48	48	50	52	52	54	58	62	64	66	68	70	72	74	76	78	82	84	88	88	92	94
IA	485	34	38	38	40	42	46	48	48	50	52	52	54	58	60	64	66	68	70	72	74	76	78	82	84	88	88	92	94
MO	486	38	38	40	40	42	44	44	46	46	48	48	50	52	54	56	56	58	60	62	64	66	66	70	72	74	74	80	80
MO	487	38	38	40	40	42	44	44	46	46	48	48	50	52	54	54	58	58	60	62	64	66	66	70	72	74	74	80	80

STATE	Area	1951	1952	1953	1954	1955	1956	1957	1958	1959	1960	1961	1962	1963	1964	1965	1966	1967	1968	1969	1970	1971	1972	1973	1974	1975	1976	1977	78
MO	488	36	38	40	40	42	44	44	46	46	48	48	50	52	52	56	56	58	60	62	64	66	66	70	72	74	74	80	80
MO	489	36	38	40	40	42	44	44	44	46	46	48	50	52	52	56	56	58	60	62	64	66	66	70	72	74	74	80	80
MO	490	36	38	38	40	42	44	44	44	46	46	48	50	52	52	54	56	58	60	62	64	64	66	70	72	74	74	78	80
MO	491	36	38	38	40	42	42	44	44	46	46	48	48	52	52	54	56	58	60	62	62	64	66	70	72	74	74	78	80
MO	492	36	38	38	40	42	44	44	44	46	46	48	48	52	52	54	56	58	60	62	62	64	66	70	72	74	74	78	80
MO	493	36	38	38	40	42	42	44	44	46	46	48	48	50	52	54	56	58	60	62	62	64	66	70	72	74	74	78	80
MO	494	36	38	38	40	42	42	44	44	46	46	48	48	52	52	54	56	58	60	60	62	64	66	70	72	74	74	78	80
MO	495	36	38	38	40	40	42	44	44	46	46	48	48	50	52	54	56	58	58	60	62	64	66	70	72	74	74	78	80
MO	496	36	36	38	38	40	42	44	44	44	46	48	48	50	52	54	56	58	58	60	62	64	66	68	72	74	74	78	80
MO	497	36	36	38	38	40	42	44	44	44	46	46	48	50	52	54	56	58	58	60	62	64	66	68	72	74	74	78	80
MO	498	36	36	38	38	40	42	44	44	44	46	46	48	50	52	54	56	58	58	60	62	64	66	68	70	74	74	78	80
MO	499	36	36	38	38	40	42	42	44	44	46	46	48	50	52	54	56	56	58	60	62	64	66	68	70	74	74	78	80
MO	500	36	36	38	38	40	42	42	44	44	46	46	48	50	52	54	56	56	58	60	62	64	66	68	70	72	72	78	78
ND	501	30	32	34	34	40	42	44	44	46	48	48	50	54	54	56	60	56	64	68	70	74	78	84	88	90	90	92	92
ND	502	32	32	32	34	36	40	42	44	44	46	48	48	50	52	54	56	58	56	62	66	70	72	76	84	86	88	92	92
SD	503	34	34	36	38	42	46	46	48	48	50	52	54	58	60	60	64	66	68	70	72	76	78	86	88	90	90	94	94
SD	504	32	34	36	36	40	44	46	46	48	50	50	54	56	58	60	62	64	66	68	72	74	76	84	86	90	90	92	92
NE	505	40	42	42	44	48	52	52	54	54	56	58	60	62	64	66	70	72	74	76	78	82	84	88	92	94	94	98	02
NE	506	38	40	42	44	46	50	52	52	54	56	56	58	64	64	66	70	72	74	76	78	80	84	88	92	94	94	98	02
NE	507	32	40	42	42	46	50	52	52	54	54	56	58	62	64	66	68	70	74	76	78	80	82	88	90	94	94	98	98
NE	508	32	40	40	42	46	50	50	52	54	54	56	58	62	64	66	68	70	72	74	78	80	82	88	90	94	94	96	98
KS	509	32	34	36	36	38	40	42	42	44	44	46	46	52	52	54	56	58	60	62	64	66	72	74	76	78	78	80	
KS	510	32	34	34	36	38	40	42	42	44	44	46	46	50	52	54	54	56	58	60	62	64	66	70	74	76	78	78	80
KS	511	32	34	34	36	38	40	40	42	42	44	46	46	50	52	52	54	56	58	60	62	64	66	70	72	74	76	78	78
KS	512	32	32	34	36	38	40	40	42	42	44	44	46	50	50	52	54	56	58	60	62	64	66	70	72	74	76	78	78
KS	513	30	32	34	34	38	40	40	42	42	44	44	46	48	50	52	54	56	58	60	62	64	64	70	72	74	76	78	78
KS	514	32	32	34	34	36	40	40	40	42	42	44	46	50	50	52	54	56	58	60	62	64	64	70	72	74	76	76	78
KS	515	32	32	34	34	36	38	40	40	42	42	44	46	48	50	52	54	56	56	58	60	62	64	70	72	74	76	76	78
MT	516	36	38	40	40	42	46	46	48	48	50	52	54	56	58	60	64	66	66	70	72	74	76	86	88	90	94	94	94
MT	517	36	36	38	40	42	44	46	46	48	50	50	52	56	58	60	62	64	66	68	70	72	74	84	88	90	92	92	92
ID	518	38	38	40	40	42	44	46	48	48	50	52	54	58	58	60	64	66	68	70	72	74	76	86	88	88	92	94	94
ID	519	36	36	38	40	42	44	44	46	48	50	52	54	56	56	60	62	64	66	70	72	74	76	84	88	90	92	94	94
WY	520	36	36	38	40	42	44	44	46	46	48	50	52	56	56	58	60	62	64	66	68	70	72	80	84	86	88	90	90

STATE	Area	1951	1952	1953	1954	1955	1956	1957	1958	1959	1960	1961	1962	1963	1964	1965	1966	1967	1968	1969	1970	1971	1972	1973	1974	1975	1976	1977	78
CO	521	42	42	46	48	50	52	52	54	56	58	60	62	66	68	72	76	78	80	84	88	90	94	02	08	13	17	21	23
CO	522	42	42	46	46	48	50	52	54	54	56	58	60	66	68	72	74	78	80	84	86	90	94	02	06	13	17	21	23
CO	523	42	42	44	46	58	50	52	52	54	56	58	60	66	68	70	74	76	80	82	86	90	94	02	06	11	17	19	23
CO	524	42	42	44	46	58	50	52	52	54	56	58	60	64	66	72	74	76	80	84	86	90	94	98	06	11	15	19	21
NM	525	74	74	80	84	86	92	96	98	98	98	98	98	98	98	98	98	98	98	98	98	98	98	08	15	19	23	25	27
AZ	526	44	44	46	48	52	54	56	60	62	64	68	72	78	80	86	90	96	02	08	17	21	27	41	51	59	65	71	75
AZ	527	42	44	46	48	50	54	56	58	60	64	66	70	74	82	84	92	96	02	08	15	21	27	41	49	57	65	69	75
UT	528	44	44	46	48	50	52	54	56	58	60	62	64	68	70	72	76	80	84	88	90	92	94	06	13	17	21	23	25
UT	529	42	44	46	48	50	52	52	54	56	58	60	64	66	70	72	76	80	84	86	88	92	94	06	11	15	19	21	25
NV	530	20	22	22	24	24	26	26	28	28	30	30	32	36	36	38	42	44	46	50	52	56	58	70	74	78	82	84	84
WA	531	32	34	34	34	38	38	40	40	40	42	44	44	48	50	52	54	56	58	60	62	64	64	70	72	74	78	80	82
WA	532	32	34	34	34	36	38	38	40	40	42	42	44	48	50	52	54	56	58	60	62	64	64	68	72	74	78	80	82
WA	533	32	32	34	34	36	38	38	40	40	42	42	44	48	48	50	54	56	58	60	60	64	64	68	72	74	78	80	82
WA	534	32	32	34	34	36	38	38	40	40	42	42	44	48	48	50	54	56	56	58	60	64	64	68	70	74	78	80	82
WA	535	32	32	32	34	36	38	38	38	40	40	42	44	46	48	50	52	54	56	60	60	62	64	68	70	74	76	80	82
WA	536	35	32	32	34	36	36	38	38	40	40	42	44	46	48	50	52	54	56	58	60	62	64	68	70	74	76	80	82
WA	537	30	32	32	34	36	36	38	38	40	42	42	44	46	48	50	52	54	56	58	60	62	64	68	70	74	76	80	82
WA	538	30	30	32	34	36	36	38	38	40	40	42	44	46	48	50	52	54	56	58	60	62	64	68	70	72	76	78	80
WA	539	30	32	32	34	36	36	38	38	40	40	42	42	46	48	50	52	54	56	58	60	62	64	68	70	72	76	78	80
OR	540	36	38	40	40	44	46	46	48	48	50	50	52	56	58	60	62	64	66	68	70	74	76	80	84	88	90	92	94
OR	541	36	38	40	40	44	44	46	46	48	48	50	52	56	58	60	62	64	66	68	72	74	76	80	84	88	90	92	94
OR	542	36	38	38	40	42	44	46	46	48	48	50	52	56	56	60	62	64	66	68	72	74	74	80	84	86	90	92	94
OR	543	36	36	38	38	42	44	44	46	46	48	50	52	54	56	58	60	64	64	68	72	74	74	80	84	86	90	92	94
OR	544	36	36	38	40	42	44	44	44	46	46	48	50	50	54	56	58	60	64	64	66	72	74	74	80	82	86	90	90	92
CA	545	46	48	50	50	52	54	56	58	60	62	64	68	72	76	80	86	88	92	98	04	11	19	27	33	39	45	49	53
CA	546	44	48	48	50	52	54	56	58	60	62	64	68	74	76	80	84	88	92	96	04	11	19	27	33	39	45	49	53
CA	547	44	46	48	50	52	54	56	58	60	62	64	66	72	76	80	84	88	92	98	02	08	19	27	33	39	45	49	53
CA	548	46	46	48	50	52	54	56	58	60	62	64	66	72	76	80	84	88	92	96	04	11	19	27	33	39	45	49	53
CA	549	46	46	48	50	52	54	56	58	60	62	64	68	72	76	80	84	88	92	96	02	08	19	27	33	39	45	49	53
CA	550	46	46	48	50	52	54	56	58	60	62	64	68	72	76	80	84	88	92	96	04	11	19	27	33	39	45	49	53
CA	551	46	46	48	50	52	54	56	58	60	62	64	68	72	76	78	84	88	92	96	02	11	17	27	33	39	45	49	53
CA	552	46	46	48	50	52	54	56	58	60	62	64	66	72	76	78	84	88	92	96	02	08	19	27	33	39	45	49	53

STATE	Area	1951	1952	1953	1954	1955	1956	1957	1958	1959	1960	1961	1962	1963	1964	1965	1966	1967	1968	1969	1970	1971	1972	1973	1974	1975	1976	1977	78
CA	553	46	46	48	50	52	54	56	58	60	60	64	66	72	76	80	82	88	92	96	02	11	19	27	33	39	43	49	53
CA	554	44	46	48	50	52	54	56	58	58	62	64	66	72	76	80	84	88	92	96	04	11	19	27	33	39	43	49	53
CA	555	44	46	48	50	52	54	56	56	58	62	64	66	72	76	80	84	88	92	96	04	11	19	27	33	37	43	49	53
CA	556	44	46	48	50	52	54	56	56	58	62	64	66	72	74	80	84	88	92	96	04	11	17	27	33	37	43	49	53
CA	557	44	46	48	50	52	54	56	56	58	62	64	66	72	74	80	82	88	92	96	02	11	17	27	33	37	43	49	53
CA	558	44	46	48	50	52	54	56	56	58	60	62	66	72	74	80	84	88	92	96	02	11	19	27	33	37	43	49	53
CA	559	44	46	48	50	52	54	56	56	58	60	64	68	70	74	80	84	86	92	96	02	08	19	27	33	37	43	49	53
CA	560	44	46	48	50	52	54	56	56	58	60	64	66	72	74	80	82	88	90	96	04	08	19	27	33	37	43	49	53
CA	561	46	46	48	50	52	54	54	56	58	60	62	66	70	74	561	82	86	92	96	02	11	19	27	33	37	43	49	53
CA	562	44	46	48	50	50	54	54	56	58	60	62	66	70	74	561	82	86	92	96	02	08	17	27	33	37	43	49	53
CA	563	44	46	48	48	50	52	54	56	58	60	62	66	70	74	80	82	86	92	94	02	08	17	27	33	37	43	49	53
CA	564	44	46	48	48	50	54	54	56	58	60	62	66	72	74	78	82	86	92	96	02	08	17	27	33	37	43	49	53
CA	565	44	46	48	48	50	52	54	56	58	60	62	66	70	74	78	82	86	90	96	02	08	17	27	33	37	43	49	53
CA	566	44	46	48	48	50	54	54	56	58	60	62	66	72	74	80	84	86	90	96	02	08	17	27	33	37	43	49	53
CA	567	44	46	48	48	50	52	54	56	58	60	62	66	72	74	78	82	88	92	96	02	08	17	27	33	37	43	49	53
CA	568	44	46	48	48	50	54	54	56	58	60	62	66	72	74	78	82	86	92	96	02	08	17	27	31	37	43	49	53
CA	569	44	46	48	48	50	52	54	56	58	60	62	66	70	74	78	82	86	92	96	02	08	17	27	31	37	43	49	53
CA	570	44	46	48	48	50	52	54	56	58	60	62	66	72	74	78	82	88	90	96	02	08	17	27	31	37	43	49	53
CA	571	44	46	46	48	50	52	54	56	58	60	62	66	72	74	78	82	86	90	96	98	08	17	27	31	37	43	47	53
CA	572	44	46	46	48	50	52	54	56	58	60	62	66	70	74	78	82	86	90	96	02	08	17	27	31	37	43	47	53
CA	573	44	46	46	48	50	52	54	56	58	60	62	66	70	74	78	82	86	90	94	02	08	17	25	31	37	43	47	53
AK	574	10	10	12	12	12	12	14	14	14	14	16	18	18	20	22	24	24	26	28	30	32	52	54	56	58	58	60	
HI	575	32	36	36	36	36	38	40	40	42	44	46	48	50	52	56	58	64	64	68	72	76	78	88	92	96	04	06	06
HI	576	30	32	32	36	36	38	38	40	42	44	44	48	50	52	54	58	60	64	66	72	74	76	88	92	96	02	04	04
DC	577	46	48	50	52	52	52	54	56	56	58	60	60	64	64	66	68	72	74	74	76	78	80	86	88	92	96	96	98
DC	578	48	46	48	50	52	52	52	54	54	56	56	58	60	62	64	66	68	70	74	74	76	78	80	86	88	92	94	96
DC	579	30	48	48	48	50	52	54	54	54	56	58	60	62	64	66	68	70	72	74	76	76	80	84	88	90	94	96	96
Virgin Islands	580	28	40	48	54	62	66	72	78	82	86	92	96	98	98	98	98	98	98	98	98	98	98	02	04	06	06	08	08
Puerto Rico	581	28	40	48	52	60	68	74	78	80	86	92	96	98	98	98	98	98	98	98	98	98	98	11	19	23	41	55	63
Puerto Rico	582		40	48	52	60	66	72	76	80	86	92	98	98	98	98	98	98	98	98	98	98	98	11	17	23	41	55	61
Puerto Rico	583												07	10	22	34	46	54	64	74	84	94	11	17	23	39	55	61	
Puerto Rico	584												03	10	18	34	40	50	62	74	84	92	08	17	23	39	55	61	
NM	585							01	05	09	12	18	26	30	38	44	50	58	66	78	88	94	08	13	19	23	25	27	

STATE	Area	1951	1952	1953	1954	1955	1956	1957	1958	1959	1960	1961	1962	1963	1964	1965	1966	1967	1968	1969	1970	1971	1972	1973	1974	1975	1976	1977	78
Guam	586					01	01	01	01	01	01	01	03	03	03	03	05	05	07	07	07	09							
Amrican Samoa							20	20	20	20	20	20	20	20	20	22	22	22	22	22	24	24							
Phillipine							30	30	30	30	30	30	30	30	30	30	30	30	30	30	30								
Islands							60	60	60	60	60	60	60	60	60	60	60	60	60	60	60	60	62	62	64	66	68	68	70
(see above)	587													05	26	46	58	74	92	98	98	98	15	19	23	27	29	31	
RR	700	18	18	18	18	18	18	18	18	18	18	18	18	18	18	18	18	18	18	18	18	18	18	18	18	18	18	18	18
RR	701	18	18	18	18	18	18	18	18	18	18	18	18	18	18	18	18	18	18	18	18	18	18	18	18	18	18	18	18
RR	702	18	18	18	18	18	18	18	18	18	18	18	18	18	18	18	18	18	18	18	18	18	18	18	18	18	18	18	18
RR	703	18	18	18	18	18	18	18	18	18	18	18	18	18	18	18	18	18	18	18	18	18	18	18	18	18	18	18	18
RR	704	18	18	18	18	18	18	18	18	18	18	18	18	18	18	18	18	18	18	18	18	18	18	18	18	18	18	18	18
RR	705	18	18	18	18	18	18	18	18	18	18	18	18	18	18	18	18	18	18	18	18	18	18	18	18	18	18	18	18
RR	706	18	18	18	18	18	18	18	18	18	18	18	18	18	18	18	18	18	18	18	18	18	18	18	18	18	18	18	18
RR	707	18	18	18	18	18	18	18	18	18	18	18	18	18	18	18	18	18	18	18	18	18	18	18	18	18	18	18	18
RR	708	18	18	18	18	18	18	18	18	18	18	18	18	18	18	18	18	18	18	18	18	18	18	18	18	18	18	18	18
RR	709	18	18	18	18	18	18	18	18	18	18	18	18	18	18	18	18	18	18	18	18	18	18	18	18	18	18	18	18
RR	710	18	18	18	18	18	18	18	18	18	18	18	18	18	18	18	18	18	18	18	18	18	18	18	18	18	18	18	18
RR	711	18	18	18	18	18	18	18	18	18	18	18	18	18	18	18	18	18	18	18	18	18	18	18	18	18	18	18	18
RR	712	18	18	18	18	18	18	18	18	18	18	18	18	18	18	18	18	18	18	18	18	18	18	18	18	18	18	18	18
Railroad	713	18	18	18	18	18	18	18	18	18	18	18	18	18	18	18	18	18	18	18	18	18	18	18	18	18	18	18	18
Retirement	714	18	18	18	18	18	18	18	18	18	18	18	18	18	18	18	18	18	18	18	18	18	18	18	18	18	18	18	18
RR	715	18	18	18	18	18	18	18	18	18	18	18	18	18	18	18	18	18	18	18	18	18	18	18	18	18	18	18	18
RR	716	18	18	18	18	18	18	18	18	18	18	18	18	18	18	18	18	18	18	18	18	18	18	18	18	18	18	18	18
RR	717	18	18	18	18	18	18	18	18	18	18	18	18	18	18	18	18	18	18	18	18	18	18	18	18	18	18	18	18
RR	718	18	18	18	18	18	18	18	18	18	18	18	18	18	18	18	18	18	18	18	18	18	18	18	18	18	18	18	18
RR	719	18	18	18	18	18	18	18	18	18	18	18	18	18	18	18	18	18	18	18	18	18	18	18	18	18	18	18	18
RR	720	18	18	18	18	18	18	18	18	18	18	18	18	18	18	18	18	18	18	18	18	18	18	18	18	18	18	18	18
RR	721	18	18	18	18	18	18	18	18	18	18	18	18	18	18	18	18	18	18	18	18	18	18	18	18	18	18	18	18
RR	722	18	18	18	18	18	18	18	18	18	18	18	18	18	18	18	18	18	18	18	18	18	18	18	18	18	18	18	18
RR	723	18	18	18	18	18	18	18	18	18	18	18	18	18	18	18	18	18	18	18	18	18	18	18	18	18	18	18	18
RR	724	18	28	28	28	28	28	28	28	28	28	28	28	28	28	28	28	28	28	28	28	28	28	28	28	28	28	28	28
RR	725	18	28	18	18	18	18	18	18	18	18	18	18	18	18	18	18	18	18	18	18	18	18	18	18	18	18	18	18
RR	726	18	18	18	18	18	18	18	18	18	18	18	18	18	18	18	18	18	18	18	18	18	18	18	18	18	18	18	18
RR	727	10	10	10	10	10	10	10	10	10	10	10	10	10	10	10	10	10	10	10	10	10	10	10	10	10	10	10	10
RR	728	09	09	18	12	12	14	14	14	14	14	14	14	14	14	14	14	14	14	14	14	14	14	14	14	14	14	14	14
RR	729	09																											

APPENDIX D

USC Title 18, Section 1028: Fraud and Related Activity in Connection with Identification Documents

~•

In order to dance around the law, you must first know it. You will also want to know what you are getting into if you decide to break the law completely (something I do not encourage or recommend). What follows is the complete text of the False Identification Crime Control Act of 1982, a/k/a Public Law 97-398. No book on the subject of identity changing or identity documents could possibly be complete without it. Now that you have a copy of this very important section of the United States Code, do yourself a favor and become familiar with it. Know what you are getting into!

Public Law 97-398-DEC. 31, 1982   96 STAT. 2009

97th Congress

An Act
To amend Title 18 of the United States Code
to provide penalties for certain
false identification related crimes.

*Be it enacted by the Senate and House of Representatives
of the United States of America in Congress assembled,* That
this Act may be cited as the "False Identification Crime
Control Act of 1982."

Sec. 2. Chapter 47 of title 18 of the United States code is
amended by adding at the end the following:

*Section 1028. Fraud and related activity in connection with
identification documents*

(a)   Whoever, in a circumstance described in subsection (c) of
this section

(1)   knowingly and without lawful authority produces
an identification document or a false identification
document;

(2)   knowingly transfers an identification document or a
false identification document knowing that such
document was stolen or produced without lawful
authority;

(3)   knowingly possesses with intent to use unlawfully
or transfer unlawfully five or more identification
documents (other than those issued lawfully for the
use of the possessor) or false identification documents;

(4)   knowingly possesses an identification document
(other than one issued lawfully for the use of the
possessor) or a false identification document, with
the intent such document be used to defraud the
United States; or

(5) knowingly produces, transfers, or possesses a document-making implement with the intent such document-making implement will be used in the production of a false identification document or another document-making implement which will be so used;

(6) knowingly possesses an identification document that is or appears to be an identification document of the United States which is stolen or produced without lawful authority knowing that such document was stolen or produced without such authority; or attempts to do so, shall be punished as provided in subsection (b) of this section.

(b) The punishment for an offense under subsection (a) of this section is

(1) a fine of not more than $25,000 or imprisonment for not more than five years, or both, if the offense is

(A) the production or transfer of an identification document or false identification document that is or appears to be

(i) an identification document issued by or under the authority of the United States; or

(ii) a birth certificate, or a driver's license or personal identification card;

(B) the production or transfer of more than five identification documents or false identification documents; or

(C) an offense under paragraph (5) of such subsection;

(2) a fine of not more than $15,000 or imprisonment for not more than three years, or both, if the offense is

(A) any other production or transfer of an identification document or false identification document; or

(B)   an offense under paragraph (3) of such
subsection; and
(3)   a fine of not more than $5,000 or imprisonment for
not more than one year, or both, in any other case.

(c) The circumstance referred to in subsection (a) of this section is that

(1)   the identification document or false identification
document is or appears to be issued by or under the
authority of the United States or the document-
making implement is designed or suited for making
such an identification document or false
identification document;

(2)   the offense is an offense under subsection (a)(4) of
this section; or

(3)   the production, transfer, or possession prohibited
by this section is in or affects interstate or foreign
commerce, or the identification document, false
identification document, or document-making
implement is transported in the mail in the course of
the production, transfer, or possession prohibited by
this section.

(d)   As used in this section

(1)   the term "identification document" means a
document made or issued by or under the authority
of the United States Government, a State, political
subdivision of a State, a foreign government,
political subdivision of a foreign government, an
international governmental or an international
quasi-governmental organization which, when
completed with information concerning a particular
individual, is of a type intended or commonly
accepted for the purpose of identification of individuals;

(2)   the term "produce" includes alter, authenticate,
or assemble;

(3)   the term "document-making implement" means any
implement or impression specially designed or

primarily used for making an identification document, a false identification document, or another document-making implement;

(4) the term "personal identification card" means an identification document issued by a State or local government solely for the purpose of identification; and

(5) the term "State" includes any State of the United States, the District of Columbia, the Commonwealth of Puerto Rico, and any other commonwealth, possession or territory of the United States.

(e) This section does not prohibit any lawfully authorized investigative, protective, or intelligence activity of a law enforcement agency of the United States, a State, or a political subdivision of a State, or of an intelligence agency of the United States, or any activity authorized under title V of the Organized Crime Control Act of 1970 (18 U.S.C. note prec. 3481).

Contacting the Author

Those who've read this book's first edition and have contacted me over the years know that I've made a point to personally answer each and every letter and e-mail I've ever received. I've since written more books, and my letter and e-mail load has grown to where I now have a public discussion forum to save myself the time of answering repeat questions.

Alas, I must report that I have decided to officially retire. I can no longer keep up the promise of answering every letter and e-mail, though I do appreciate the thoughtful comments and suggestions. Indeed they have helped shape this revised edition.

I will still read my e-mails and will reply when time allows, especially if a reader raises a point not covered in my discussion forum or in one of my books. Chances are, I'll reply in the discussion forum so all may benefit. It's probably best just to post your important questions there in the first place, as other contributors may have already dealt with the issue and could offer insight that I may not be able to.

I seldom post to the forum myself anymore because I now travel quite frequently. But I do occasionally check in. For the most part, the group seems to do well on its own.

You can link to the discussion forum via my Web site:

www.phreak.co.uk/sxc

• ⤳

This Web address may change from time to time, but you can always find me by visiting Paladin Press' Web site at www.paladin-press.com and finding my site listed under "Author Links."

Thank you to all who have supported me over the years.

—Sheldon Charrett,
anchored 260 mi. ESE of Charlotte, SC, June 2003